VOLUME THREE

SOLDAT

THE WORLD WAR II GERMAN ARMY COMBAT UNIFORM COLLECTOR'S HANDBOOK

EQUIPPING THE GERMAN FOOT SOLDIER IN EUROPE, 1944–1945

by CYRUS A. LEE

PICTORIAL HISTORIES PUBLISHING CO.
Missoula, Montana

LIBRARY OF CONGRESS
CATALOG CARD NO. 90-64461

ISBN 0-929521-46-3

First Printing: March 1991
Second Printing: April 1993

Photography by Cyrus Lee and Christoph Schafer
Grammatical Editing by Dave Clausen, Shirley Harryman
and Jacquelyn McGiffert
Photolayouts by Cyrus Lee, Christoph Schafer and Georg Schafer
Small Arms Research and Text by John Milejski
Lernen durch Erfahrung Research and Text by Mark Watts

Companion Volume:

Vol. II - Equipping the German Army Foot Soldier
in Europe 1943

Future Companion Volumes:

Vol. I - Equipping the German Army Foot Soldier
in Europe 1939-1942
Vol. IV - Equipping the German Army Foot Soldier in
Southern Europe and North Africa 1940-1945
Vol. V - Uniforms and Insignia of Panzerkorps
Grossdeutschland
Vol. VI - Uniforms and Insignia of the Waffen SS
Panzer Regiments 1942-1945
Vol. VII - Uniforms and Insignia of the Waffen SS
Panzer-Grenadier Regiments 1939-1945

Pictorial Histories Publishing Co., Inc.
713 South Third Street
Missoula, Montana 59801

Preface

*S*oldat, Volume III, continues to meet the basic needs of those who collect German Army combat uniforms and equipment. First, I have continued to provide clear and educational descriptions of the uniforms and equipment of the German foot soldier.

Second, I have increased the number, the detail, and the clarity of the photos of the uniforms and equipment of the German foot soldier of 1944 and 1945. The photographs displayed in *Soldat* are not static historical documents, but are chosen to create a feeling of being part of the total historical experience of this time and place - the German Army front lines.

Third, through *"Der alte Hase,"* I have continued to include an aspect of collecting that is so often left out - the soldier's side of the story.

The years 1944 and 1945 have been chosen as the theme of this volume because of their extreme importance in the history of the German foot soldier. These were the ending years of the conflict and were the years which found the German foot soldier locked in a fighting retreat on all fronts of the European Continent. These years marked the high tide of German military production and technological advancement. In 1944 and 1945 the foot soldier received new types of uniforms, equipment and weapons.

The early years of spectacular triumphs were now forgotten and survival was the watchword of the soldier. Desperate counter attacks of late 1944 provided momentary hope of salvation for the German people. However, the "total war" declared by the Allies continued to grind closer to each soldier's home, until the end came in 1945.

This work is about the uniforms and equipment of the German Army foot soldier who fought in Europe in 1944 and 1945. *Soldat* continues to tell about the individual German soldier, how he dressed, the things he carried, the weapons he fought with, the food he ate, and the life he lived.

Introduction

*T*his volume of *Soldat* is divided into three chapters, each dealing with a special area of the uniforms, equipment and weapons of the German foot soldier in Europe in 1944 and 1945. There is a new portion of the equipment chapter called "*Lernen durch Erfahrung*" or "*Training Through Experience*" that will help the collector find production codes and markings.

The arrangement of the photos and text is such that the reader can easily go from one to the other without losing place. The Table of Contents enables the reader to quickly find the exact item in print and photo.

There is an index to *Der alte Hase* located at the rear of the book for easy reference to a unique source of information.

Located in the appendix is <u>The *Soldat* Combat Uniform Collector's Planner</u>. By making copies of and using the <u>Planner</u>, the reader can better organize his or her collection.

Soldat is a handbook for collectors of German Army combat uniforms and equipment. *Soldat* has been created from the research of historical and contemporary writings, interviews with veterans of the German Army, and photographs of items in individual collections.

Acknowledgments

*T*hese people put in the time and effort that is essential for the completion of a project such as this volume of *Soldat*. Their help deserves recognition and thanks!

For sharing their memories, photos, stories and time; I give my thanks to the veterans of the German Army of 1939-1945.

For the use of their collections for photos and study; I give my thanks to:
Christoph Schafer
Georg Schafer
Jens Link
Josef Witt
Hayes Otoupalik
Mark Pegram
Mark Watts
T. Walpurgius
Die Wehrtechnische Studiensammlung, Koblenz, Germany
Diekirch Historical Museum, Diekirch, Luxembourg
Museum Hurtgenwald '44, Kleinhau/Duren, Germany

For their help with key information, documentation, translation, support, and research, I give my thanks to:
Kim Lee
Dave Clausen
Christoph Schafer
Georg Schafer
Josef Witt
Richard Mundt
Hans Blache
John Milejski
Mark Watts
Uli Brodner

Herr Heinrich, Wehrtechnische Studiensammlung
Roland Schall, Museum Hurtgenwald'44
Roland Gaul, Diekirch Historical Museum
Kevin Poole

For giving their time and for standing very still under difficult circumstances, my thanks to the photomodels:
John Milejski
Richard Mundt
Jens Link
Mark Pegram
Charles
William Ramsey
Ted Nelsen
Bob Laabs

For continued support in publishing and sales, my thanks to: Stan and Leslie of Pictorial Histories Publishing Co.

For your letters, suggestions, and morale boosting, I thank you, the collectors, historians, model builders, and everyone else who has bought, read, and enjoyed *Soldat*!

I am continuing to seek comments and input on this and future volumes of *Soldat*. I have been very pleased with the input that I have received to date. Nearly all of the comments have been critically constructive in nature, and have helped me to develop the direction of future volumes of *Soldat*. Only through your comments and suggestions can I tailor *Soldat* to your needs and desires! Your letters do not fall into a forgotten pile, unread. I have strived to answer each of your questions by return post, and I will strive to continue to do so.

I am seeking uniforms, equipment and weapons for inclusion in future volumes of *Soldat*. These future volumes will include books on: the Waffen SS Panzer-Grenadiers, the Afrika Korps and tropical uniforms, and the German Airborne Forces. If you are interested in participating in the creation of these volumes, please contact me.

Please send all correspondence through Pictorial Histories Publishing Co., 713 So. Third, Missoula, MT 59801, USA.

Cyrus A. Lee

Table of Contents

An alte kampfer waits for the enemy. The bushy hedgerows are his comrades.

Normandy 1944

For the soldiers of my platoon, June, July, and August of 1944 were a lifetime lived in three months. Our 2nd Company was part of the 1056 Regiment, one of the infantry regiments of the 89th Infantry Division. We were deployed in Normandy.

The first thing one has to notice about Normandy in the summer is that it is very green. Spring leaves Normandy with lush fields of grass, fruit trees coming ripe with fruit, and very warm. The fields of Normandy are full of white dairy cows that are covered with black or brown spots. Each morning and evening these cows deliver milk that is, for the most part, made into delicious cheeses. The orchards of apple trees produce fruit that becomes cider and Calvados liquor. Orchards and fields are separated with tall hedgerows. These hedgerows are a tangle of roots and growth that hold the soil in ever-growing wall-like structures. Each year as the trees of the hedge grow, the farmer plows and harvests. This removal and change of the soil lowers the level of the field downward. After hundreds of years the result is a stout fence between properties. Many of these properties are only one hundred meters square and have very different elevations. Normandy, being near the sea, has a humid climate that causes the sweat to stick to the body and in turn dirt to stick to the sweat. When the weather is clear, and it is mostly clear in the summer, the blue sky seems to climb higher than the sun. The sun, however, seems to always place itself right on top of the soldier's helmet.

It was into this type of weather that the Allies launched the attack to relieve our pressure on their Russian allies. The repulsion of this invasion was our reason for being in Normandy. We had some time to enjoy the benefits of the Norman countryside, but for the most part the natural elements were our enemies. The weapon most feared by the infantry soldier is enemy air power. The bright blue, clear, Norman sky allowed the Allied "Jabos" (soldier slang for fighter-bomber) to constantly remain above our front lines to hunt for unwary soldiers and vehicles. The "Jabos" did their works of death unencumbered by our own fighters, who put in few appearances. The long summer days allowed the "Jabos" to inhibit our movement until the night.

The short nights were not a time of peace for us. During the night all work and movement had to be carried out. When fighting was going on by day, and work and movement by night, the soldier had little or no time for sleep. In the six hours or so of darkness, we had to send our wounded to the rear, resupply our munitions, food and drink, and ensure our positions were ready for the enemy attacks in the morning. If our company had to move in or out of the line, we would march all night and then occupy new positions. After days of this type of sleepless existence, one's life is not normal. Without sleep it is hard to make decisions; the nerves are easily unravelled; tempers flare. Perhaps the most dangerous part of the lack of sleep is that your body may overcome your will or fear and go to sleep anyway, very likely in a place of great danger. This type of existence also precludes the washing of the body and all but basic care of equipment. Even the First Sergeant becomes unconcerned with everything but the basic needs of the company.

The long, sunny, hot days require that a soldier conserve his water ration, if he has gotten any in the first place. With constant enemy observation it is not possible to just go fetch some water as needed. A movement like this could bring down the "Jabos" on the whole platoon. Fortunately, the nature of our fighting in Normandy allowed, actually required, us to hide our positions in the hedgerows. This provided some relief from the sun on top of our steel helmets.

The hedgerows provided us with valuable obstacles to block the advance of the enemy armor and this made their infantry attack us on equal terms. We would let squads hold adjacent sections of hedgerows. The squad sergeant would ensure that his squad's weapons were covering all enemy access routes into these sections. In order to make sure that the squad could escape if enemy pressure was too great, escape routes to the next defensive position were laid out. To provide maximum effectiveness of our weapons, the gunners and leaders always tried to measure and mark ranges of engagement. Our company mortars were also ranged in advance on predetermined targets to support our defense or cover our withdrawal to our next position.

The hedgerows are taller than a standing man and you can

not see through them easily. This lack of a distant horizon makes getting disoriented very easy. We used this to our advantage as often as possible by popping up and firing on advancing enemy troops from their flank. Sometimes this caused them to change the course of their attack and possibly engage their own comrades! This advantage of the hedgerows also made it difficult for the enemy to radio in for support by the "Jabos" because the enemy leaders often did not know where they actually were. Unfortunately for us, the enemy could overcome this difficulty with the use of colored smoke grenades. Because we had marked out our routes through the hedgerows, we were normally unaffected by the disorientation problem.

The hedgerows were also to our benefit when the enemy employed armor in his assaults. As a tank climbed the hedgerow, its soft underbelly was exposed and its weapons were ineffective. These two advantages allowed us to employ our Panzerfausts and Panzerschrecks with great success. This advantage was offset when the Americans attached devices to the front of their tanks that allowed them to dig into the hedgerow and then push it over. This new American device required that our tank-hunting teams be more skillful in their attacks. No longer were they assured a defenseless target as the tank's weapons all remained in action. American tanks could be defeated by any shot into the vehicle body, so our tank hunters now aimed for the tank's side or rear. The American tanks usually caught fire when hit, causing the surviving crew members to abandon the vehicle and expose themselves to our weapons. The enemy infantry and armor troops were very cautious in their assaults on our positions in the hedgerows.

The enemy's superiority in numbers and firepower slowly pushed us out of the Normandy. Our withdrawal found us fighting for our lives in the "Devil's Cauldron" (Falaise Pocket). We cheated the Angel of Death and the prison camps by getting through the "Corridor of Death" and crossing the River Dives at Moissy. What was left of our regiment crossed the Seine River and carried on into Belgium and Germany for rest and refitting. The Americans outran their supply lines, and the British took the fight into Holland. In September we found ourselves in the mountains south of Aachen. Our regiment was 350 men strong. We hoped for a period of rest and a chance to get and train replacements. The Americans had different ideas for the area we were occupying.

These soldiers are enjoying a quiet moment in the hedgerows.

The Uniform

A decorated "alte Hase" wears a **Service Tunic Model 43**. He is armed with a **Panzerfaust 60M** and is wearing a **Magazine Pouch** for the MP43/StG44.

The Service Tunic Model 1943

In 1944 and 1945 the Service Tunic Model 1943 (M43) was the standard of issue to the German foot soldier. The M43 was a major deviation from the previous Service Tunic Model 1936 in both appearance and materials of manufacture. With the precedent for removal of the dark green collar and shoulder boards set by the war time production variant (this Service Tunic variant was produced from 1940 until the M43 took its place.

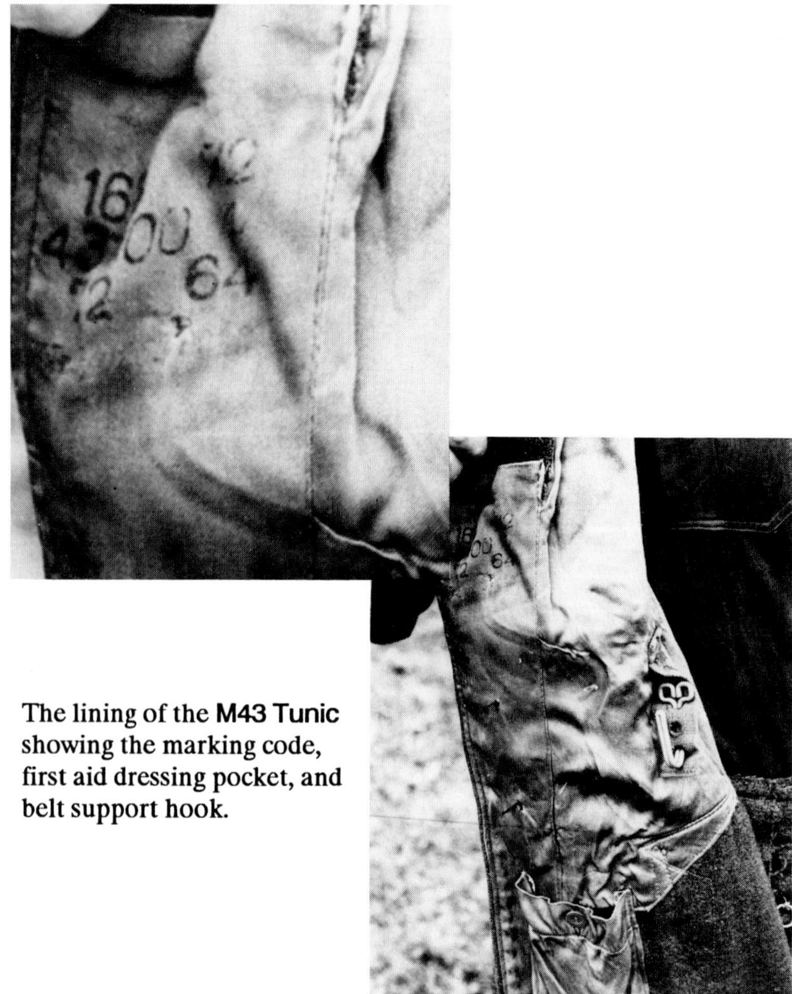

The lining of the **M43 Tunic** showing the marking code, first aid dressing pocket, and belt support hook.

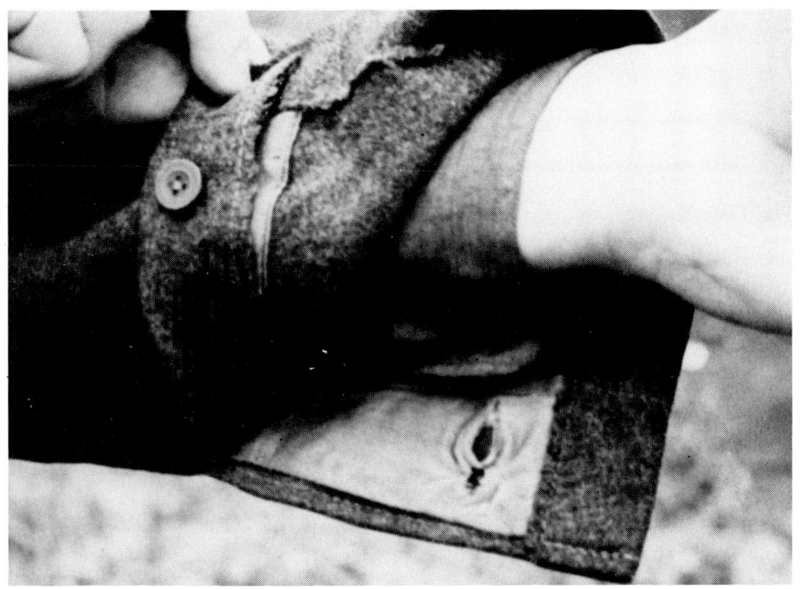

Details of the sleeve cuff interior of the **M43 Tunic**. Of special note is the pressed paper button.

This Service Tunic variant is sometimes referred to as the M40 pattern) of the M36 Service Tunic, further changes were a matter of course for an economy straining to produce at a "total war" pace.

The M43 was linked in appearance to the M36 or M40 only in that it had four, pleatless, patch pockets with button-down flaps, pebbled fieldgrey metal buttons and shoulder boards. The pocket flaps lost their scalloped bottoms and became rectangular in appearance. Another button was added to secure the tunic front, increasing the total to six fieldgrey, pebbled buttons. The M43 could be closed at the collar with a metal hook and ring, or worn "open."

The early productions of the M43 had a artificial cotton or linen lining, such as that seen on the M36 or M40. As production continued, these linings gave way to artificial silk. The M43 lost the internal support yoke that had been designed into the M36 and the M40. The cartridge belt support hooks were now retained with the use of adjustable, artificial-silk straps with reinforced eyelets, sewn into the tunic sides. The first aid dressing pocket was sewn into the lining at the lower right corner of the tunic front flap, secured with a plastic or pressed-paper button. The pressed-paper buttons were stamped from plastic-impregnated cardboard, making them more durable than they sound.

The color of the M43 also changed, due to two major factors. First, the wool used in manufacture was recycled, reworked for use in the tunic fabric. This recycled wool was already colored in various tones of fieldgrey. Second, the "spun-rayon" yarn content of the cloth was much higher than that of any other previous uniform fabric. The combination of the recycled wool and the rayon produced a harder, stone-grey color rather than the warm green of the earlier tunics.

All factory-produced uniform insignia were executed in fieldgrey and mouse-grey artificial silk. This included the national eagle/swastika symbol and the collar tabs, which were directly sewn, without backing, onto the tunic.

Shoulder boards were attached to the M43 by means of a cloth loop at the shoulder sleeve joint and a pebbled metal button on the shoulder. The shoulder boards were normally of the same cloth as the M43 with the appropriate branch color sewn in. However, any style of shoulder board could be used, and earlier models manufactured in dark green cloth, usually from the foot soldier's previous tunic, found their way onto the M43 Service Tunic.

This Senior Private is wearing a worn **Service Tunic Model 1943**. This soldier is wearing his **Cartridge Belt** without any equipment, perhaps he is home on leave. More details found in Vol. II.

The details of the front portion of the **Model 1943 Belted Trouser.**

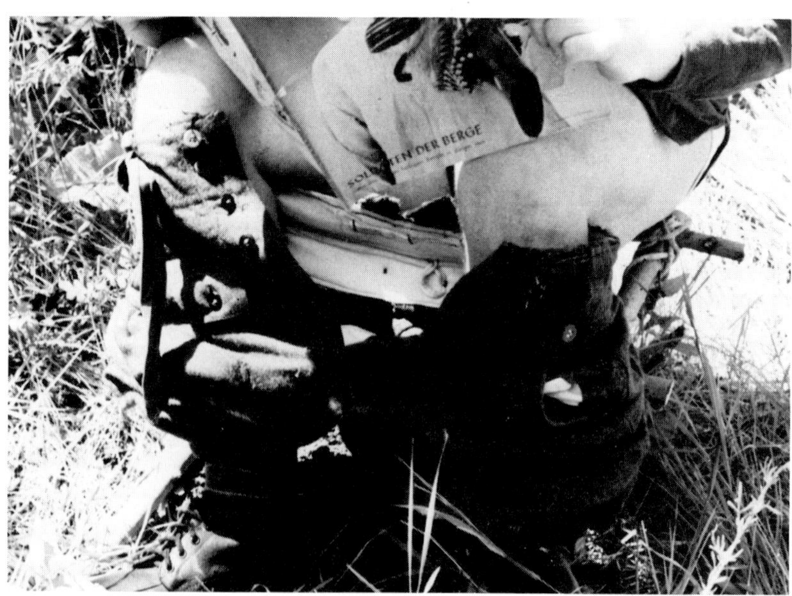

The interior details of the **Model 1943 Belted Trouser.**

The Model 1943 Belted Trouser

The adoption of the "Mountain-style" trouser by the German Army had provided a step of practicality in the right direction. However, the need for a trouser with a totally organic support system other than suspenders still existed. The use of the standard Cartridge-Belt was not sufficient to hold up the trousers and the lack of an issue trouser belt bedeviled the foot soldier when he was required to use the Cartridge Belt for its proper purpose. To this end all manners of belts were tried, including rope. Not only were these inconvenient and against regulation, but also they were easily lost due to the large size and low number of the belt loops affixed to the "Mountain-style" trouser.

Experience with uniform trousers in North Africa brought the development of the Model 1943 Belted Trouser. Officially adopted in June of 1943, the M43 trouser began to make its impact on the comfort of troops in late 1943 and early 1944.

The details of the front of the **Model 1943 Belted Trouser.** Of interest is the tapered trouser leg and the strap used to hold the bloused trouser leg inside the boot and gaiter.

The key new feature of the Model 1943 Belted Trouser was the inclusion of an organic fabric belt into the design. The cloth belt ran through a tunnel in the waistband of the trouser and was fastened by use of a two-pronged metal buckle. Four large, button down belt loops were provided to support the Cartridge Belt when the trousers were worn in "shirt sleeve order."

The M43 Belted Trouser was produced in fieldgrey cloth and was lined with artificial cotton or linen. The M43 retained the two flapped front side pockets, the watch pocket with flap and metal ring, and one flapped rear pocket. These pockets and the fly were secured with buttons of either artificial horn, plastic or metal. The design of the trouser leg was like that of the "Mountain-style" trouser and retained the tapered, slashed bottom with securing straps. The M43 Belted Trouser did not have the reinforced seat that the "Mountain-style" trouser had. For those who mistrusted the belt; or who were of more of a traditional mind, plastic, artificial horn or metal suspender buttons were retained inside the waistband of the trouser.

The details of the rear of the **Model 1943 Belted Trouser.**

How to Read the Uniform Marking Codes 1944-1945

In general, all uniform pieces are factory marked on the inside, usually in black indelible ink. The purpose of this stamping is to show origin of production and the size of the uniform piece.

Included in the uniform marking codes, beginning at the end of 1942, was the RB number. The RB numbers reflected a coded number that represented manufacturers on a national scale. The RB number was to replace the manufacturer's stamp.

After the beginning of 1943, the marking codes generally did not reflect the manufacturer, and sometimes, the depot of issue and the year which the uniform item was received. The depot code stamp reflected the probable year of manufacture for that item. The depot was denoted in the code by the first letter of the depot's name. The year the item was received by the depot was shown in the code by its last two digits. This depot code was placed below the sizing information codes.

Below is an example of marking codes of a Field Service Tunic produced in 1940. These codes are located on the uniform's right side, above the field dressing pocket:

43 · 44
100
72 · 64
F 40

The 43 indicates the length of the tunic back.

The 44 indicates the tunic collar size.

The 100 indicates the tunic chest size.

The 72 indicates the overall tunic length.

The 64 indicates the tunic sleeve length.

The F indicates the depot in Frankfurt.

The 40 indicates the year the tunic was received by the depot in Frankfurt.

After the beginning of 1943 the marking codes for the Field Service Tunic did not always contain the depot code stamp. An example of the marking codes for a Model 1943 Field Service Tunic:

RB Nr. 0/0375/0025

45 · 46
104
74 · 68

The RB Nr. 0/0375/0025 is the manufacturer.
The 45 indicates the length of the tunic back.
The 46 indicates the tunic collar size.
The 104 indicates the tunic chest size.
The 74 indicates the overall tunic length.
The 68 indicates the tunic sleeve length.

The marking codes for the greatcoat are the same as for the tunic except that they are marked on the coat's left side. In the case of a greatcoat with a lining, the code may be located within the left inside pocket. The overall length of the greatcoat will be reflected in a number proportionately larger than that of a Field Service Tunic.

The general marking codes for all service trousers produced after the start of 1943 and prior to the production of the Model 1944 Field Service Trouser were all of the same pattern. This is an example of the marking codes for the Model 1943 Belted Trouser. These codes are normally found on the right side of the trouser waistband:

RB Nr. 0/0354/0010

78 · 80
111 · 96

The RB Nr. 0/03540/0010 indicates the manufacturer.
The 78 indicates the trouser inseam length.
The 80 indicates the trouser waist size.

The 111 indicates the overall trouser length.
The 96 indicates the trouser seat size.

The marking code for the Model 1944 Field Service Tunic was not always the same as that of Model 1943 Service Tunic. The codes for the M44 could be displayed in two different manners, either horizontally, as with other tunics; or vertically. The codes were always to be stamped on the tunic's left side between the third and fourth button.

This is an example of the vertical placement of the marking codes for a Field Service Tunic Model 1944:

RB Nr 0/0634/0020

76
39
84
41
59

The RB Nr. 0/0634/0020 indicates the manufacturer.
The 76 indicates the tunic sleeve length.
The 39 indicates the tunic collar size.
The 84 indicates the tunic chest size.
The 41 indicates the tunic back length.
The 59 indicates the overall tunic length.

The marking codes used for the Model 1944 Field Service Trouser were different from the marking codes used on other service trousers. The code on the M44 trousers did not contain the overall trouser length. This is an example of a marking code for the Model 1944 Field Service Trouser:

RB Nr. 0/0514/0300
68 · 74
90

The RB Nr. 0/0514/0300 indicates the manufacturer.
The 68 indicates the trouser inseam length.

The 74 indicates the trouser waist size.
The 90 indicates the trouser seat size.

All sizes are noted in centimeters. By no means do all uniform pieces contain all the information shown above. Wear and cleaning remove many types of inks; therefore, some of the marking code information may be missing.

This "alte Hase" has sewn his old pattern collar insignia on to this **Model 1944 Field Service Tunic.** The tunic has the last triangular pattern National Insignia.

The Model 1944 Field Service Tunic

The Model 1944 Field Service Tunic (M44) was the final pattern of service tunic developed for the German foot soldier during the Second World War. The search for a more practical service tunic, which could be produced at a more economical and faster rate, began in 1943 and culminated with the official introduction of the M44 on the 25th of September 1944. The acceptance of the M44 was the final break from the traditionally

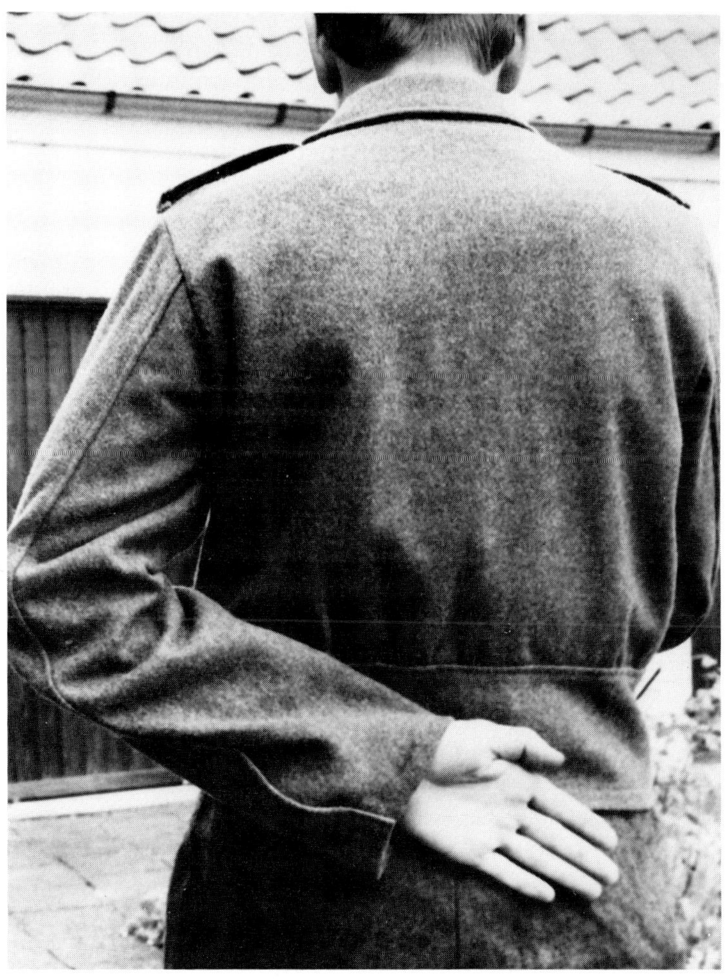

The details of the back of the **Model 1944 Field Service Tunic.**

styled tunic of the German foot soldier.

The first samples of the Model 1944 Field Service Tunic were issued on a trial basis in the summer of 1943. The M44 and other uniform items were issued to and evaluated by the 17th Infantry Division, the 73rd Infantry Division, the 78th Assault Division, the 28th Light-Infantry Division, the 104th Light-Infantry Division, the 2nd Mountain Division, the 16th Armored Division, and the Replacement Brigade for the Armored Infantry Division "Grossdeutschland". These units reported the results of the trials on the M44 to the General Staff. The input of these units was taken into account, and after design changes the new pattern was shown to Hitler on 8 July 1944.

The late date of issue, distribution to only newly raised or reconstituting units, and the required exhaustion of present stocks of earlier models of service tunics lessened the impact the M44 made on the appearance of the German field army. The Model 1944 Field Service Tunic closely resembled the British Battle Dress Blouse. Since the tunic was cut short, the bottom pockets of the earlier German service tunics were eliminated; only two upper patch pockets, with flaps secured with metal, pebbled buttons remained. The top of the tunic was gathered into a broad waist band, which held the tunic snugly over the top of the service trouser. The M44 was closed with six metal, pebbled buttons, often secured by metal split clips or s-rings. Although the collar could be buttoned closed, it was usually worn open.

The sleeve-cuff of the **Model 1944 Field Service Tunic** could be adjusted by means of two button holes cut directly into the sleeve material.

The interior details of the **Model 1944 Field Service Tunic**. Of special interest is the marking code and the interior pocket.

The lining of the M44 was usually of artificial cotton and contained two interior pockets. The four cartridge-belt support hooks in previous tunic designs now gave way to two, supported by straps with up to five adjustment holes or slits sewn in. The openings for these hooks in the tunic sides were reduced in number to one on each side.

Two button holes at the wrists made the sleeves of the M44 Service Tunic adjustable. The buttons and others inside were made of plastic, pressed paper or rubberized paper. Later modifications to the M44 Service Tunic removed the pocket flaps, changed the sleeve adjustment design, modified the waistband and removed the cartridge-belt support straps.

The Model 1944 Field Service Tunic was to be produced from uniform cloth that contained a high percentage of "spun rayon" yarn mixed with a small amount of recycled wool material. This new uniform cloth was more olive green than the fieldgrey cloth used in earlier service tunics. This new shade of material was called "Fieldgrey 44". Production orders required that all existing stocks of older fieldgrey cloth were to be exhausted first, and the M44 was produced in a variety of shades of fieldgrey. Shoulder boards used for the tunic could be of the same shade as the tunic or of other manufacture and design. The shoulder boards were held in place by a cloth loops and metal, pebbled buttons.

The woven national eagle/swastika insignia and collar tabs for the M44 were executed in field grey and mousegrey artificial silk, produced on a new triangular pattern base. The final national insignia version was embroidered, the eagle/swastika details were placed on an artificial cotton base which was then sewn to the tunic. However, older patterns of the national insignia were used in place of the new styles as well.

The triangular regulation National Insignia normally seen on the **M44.**

The Model 1944 Field Service Trouser

The Model 1944 Field Service Trouser was the final style of trouser produced for the foot soldier and was designed for use with the Model 1944 Field Service Tunic.

The Model 1944 Field Service Trouser design made use of the organic cloth belt as used in the M43 Belted Trouser; here the majority of similarities ended. The M44 trouser received an additional rear button-down pocket with a flap to go with the front and rear pockets traditionally placed on the service trousers. The cloth support loops for wearing of the Cartridge Belt when in "shirt-sleeve order" were increased from four to six. The internal cloth belt was secured with either a two- or three-prong metal buckle or by a metal double-ring friction buckle. The M44 trouser legs were not tapered, and a draw string was incorpo-

Details of the front of the **Model 44 Field Service Trouser** and **Belt.**

Details of the rear of the **M44 Trouser.**

rated inside the seam to blouse the cuff with the Short Lace-up Ankle Boot with or without Canvas Gaiter. The traditional suspender positioning buttons were kept in position even though, in theory, the internal cloth belt would keep the trouser in its correct position.

The Model 1944 Field Service Trouser was to be produced from the same "Fieldgrey 44" uniform cloth as the M44 Field Service Tunic. Production orders required that existing stocks of fieldgrey uniform cloth be depleted before the new "Fieldgrey 44" uniform cloth could be used. Therefore, M44 trousers were produced of whatever material was on hand in the factory. The trousers were lined with artificial cotton fabric. The buttons used for securing the pockets, fly, and suspenders were made of plastic or metal.

As with the Model 1944 Field Service Tunic, the M44 Field Service Trouser was not widely distributed to the German foot soldier and was issued only to newly raised or reconstituting units and when other stores were exhausted.

Cover and Protect the Wound

Each foot soldier was issued and was required to carry two Field First Aide Dressings. These dressings were of the compress bandage design, which was placed firmly over the wound and then secured by attached, fabric ties. The soldier was issued two bandages because wounds caused by fully jacketed military bullets normally have entry and exit points.

The soldier was issued two sizes of first aide dressings. The smaller of the dressing packet was about two centimeters (3/4 inch) thick, four centimeters (1-1/2 inches) wide and eight centimeters (3-1/4 inches) long. When taken out of the package, the dressing unfolded to cover an area of about eight centimeters (3-1/4 inches) by twelve centimeters (4-3/4 inches). The larger bandage was issued in a package measuring about three centimeters (1-1/4 inches) thick, seven centimeters (2-3/4 inches) wide and ten centimeters (4 inches) long. When removed from

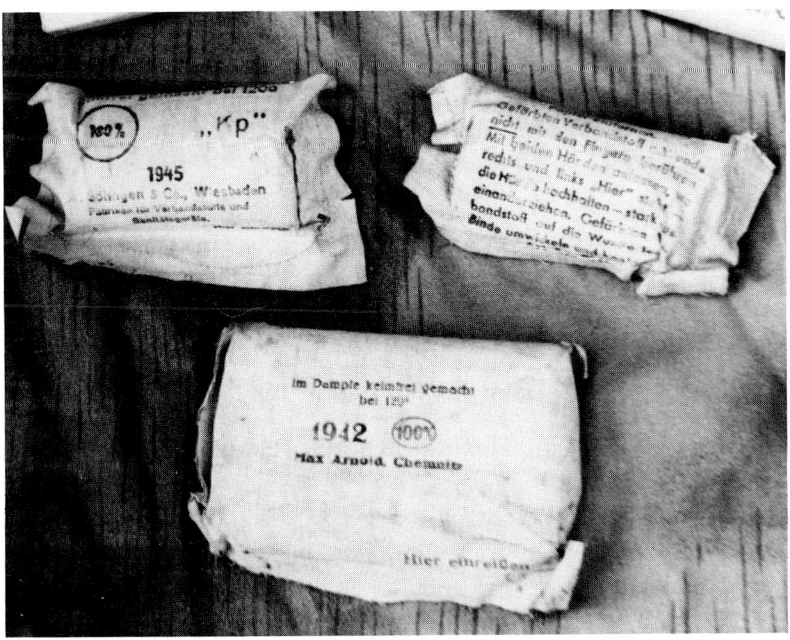

Each soldier carried two **Field First Aid Dressings**. Shown here are two small dressings and one large dressing.

When the **Field First Aid Dressing** package is opened, the dressing can be unfolded and put in place. Of interest is the "HEIR" stamp on the dressing and the sterile wrapping paper.

the package the dressing unfolded to cover an area of about ten centimeters (4 inches) by twenty-one centimeters (8-1/4 inches). The soldier was issued the two sizes of dressings because bullet wounds usually have a small entry point with a large exit point.

The dressings produced during the war period were heat sealed inside a sanitary, water-proof case of rubberized fabric. The bandage was protected from soiled hands by a paper wrapper, tied and folded around the fabric. The bandage ties were marked with the word "HERE" to indicate the position for proper handling in order to preserve the sterility of the bandage surface. The ties and sterile surface were kept closed by another string tie, which was snapped off when the bandage was opened.

The Field First Aid Dressings were carried in a small pouch sewn into the right, lower front corner of the Service Tunic and HBT Service Tunic Model 1943. The dressings were carried in the right interior pocket of the Model 1944 Field Service Tunic. Soldiers would often also carry spare dressings in the Gasmask Canister.

Wounded soldiers usually get their first help from a comrade who applied the field bandages to the wounds and then attempted to get a medic to render further assistance. As a rule the bandages of the wounded man, not those of the helper were used. If the wounded man could move, he would either continue on with the squad or he would be sent to the battalion aid station. If the man was unable to move, he would have to wait for a stretcher.

Depending upon the severity of the wound, the soldier may have found himself either returned to his unit in a short time or he may have received a ticket home. However, any hospital along his path could pronounce him fit for duty and return him to the front. By 1944 and 1945, many periods of convalescent leave ended abruptly. If a soldier knew he was going to be pronounced fit for combat soon after his wound, he knew he had only eight weeks from the time of his injury to secure a release from the hospital. Otherwise he would be sent into the Replacement Army for reassignment to a new unit, and would be permanently separated from old friends and comrades.

The Model 1943 Field Cap

The Model 1943 Field Cap was the most popular field cap issued to the German forces during the conflict. The M43 Field Cap became a symbol of the German Army of the Second World War.

The M43 cap was patterned after the cap issued to mountain troops. The differences between the M43 cap and the Mountain Cap were that the M43 had a slightly longer bill, had no interior leather sweatband, and had the fieldgrey material of the same poor quality as the Service Uniform Model 1943. It had the same fold-down side flap as the M42 Field Cap.

The **Model 1943 Field Cap** with sides folded down to protect the ears and face during cold weather.

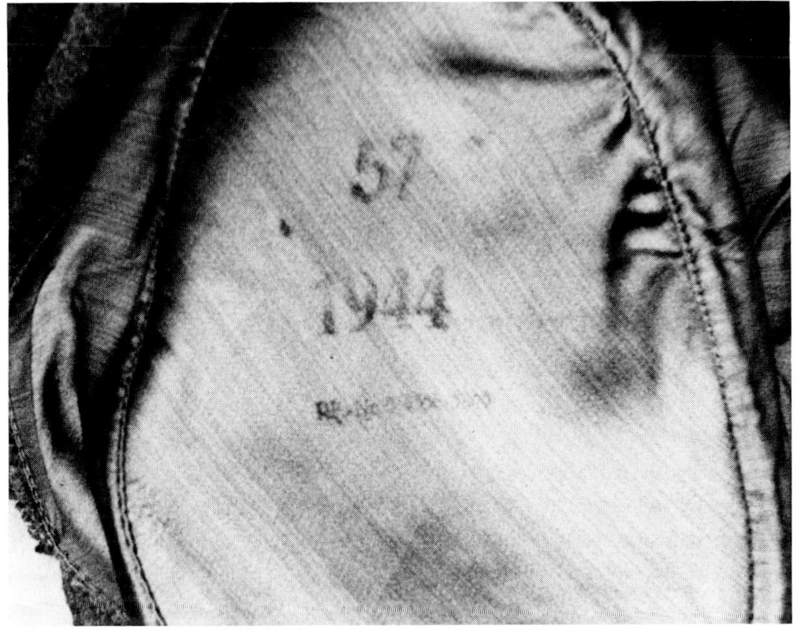

The interior of the **Model 1943 Field Cap**. Of interest are the size, production date, and RB Number stamped inside. More details can be found in Vol. II.

The national insignia was woven in red, white and black or mousegrey on a fieldgrey artificial silk background. The insignia was executed in either a T- or trapezoid-shaped design and sewn directly to the cap.

The M43 Field Cap was provided with metal-reinforced ventilation holes, one on either side. The cap was lined with either grey artifical cotton or artificial silk.

The Model 1943 Field Cap was the final pattern of field cap issued to the German Army. By 1945, the majority of uniforms of the German foot soldier included the M43 cap.

The Model 1935 Steel Helmet

The German foot soldier began the Second World War with the Model 1935 Steel Helmet. In 1944 and 1945 this helmet was still in use. The M35 helmet was produced with the helmet edge rim folded down and inward in order to provide a smooth finish to the helmet construction. It was produced in versions with one or two decals or in a version with no decals at all and was painted in varied shades of green or fieldgrey. The M35 helmet's outer finish changed from a pre-war smooth texture to a rougher wartime texture in order to reduce the risk of surface glare.

The Model 1935 Steel Helmet had a leather liner that was suspended inside the helmet shell from steel and aluminum bands. A two piece leather chin strap was provided to secure the helmet on the head.

In 1940, a slight modification was made in the production of the M35 Pattern Steel Helmet. In order to reduce construction time and cost, the separate vent hole reinforcing washers were eliminated in favor of stamped in dimpled ring.

A moment's pause. This sergeant is wearing a
Model 1935 Steel Helmet.

The Model 1942 Steel Helmet

The Model 1942 Steel Helmet differed in construction from the M35 Steel Helmet in one very noticeable way: the helmet edge was not crimped into a roll around the rim, but rather flared outward and was left rough. This new construction style gave the M42 a slightly larger appearance and tended to cut through helmet covers. It was produced in versions usually with a single decal or with no decal and was painted varied shades of green or fieldgrey with a dull finish.

The helmet liner and chin strap were the same as those of the M35 helmet. As the conflict moved into the late war years, the M42 Steel Helmet became the predominant helmet of the German foot soldier.

This corporal is wearing a **Model 1942 Steel Helmet.** More details can be found in Vol. I or Vol. II.

The Camouflage Helmet Cover

The Camouflage Helmet Cover was fashioned from five pieces of cloth sewn together to fit the contours of the steel helmet. Seven cloth loops were sewn onto the cover for the purpose of holding natural camouflage materials. Versions of the cover exist without these loops. The cover was held in position on the helmet by means of a drawstring around the free edge.

The first camouflage covers were manufactured from artifical twill cloth printed in the Army Splinter Camouflage Pattern. Later, covers were produced from artifical cotton cloth in both of the Army camouflage patterns.

Camouflage covers were also produced in the field from varying camouflage materials such as Shelter Quarters. Field-made helmet covers were produced in the style of the Waffen SS helmet cover, too. This design used metal rocker clips to hold the cover on the helmet.

Details of the **Camouflage Helmet Cover.** Of interest is the five section construction and the placement of the camouflage loops. Other details can be found in Vol. I and Vol. II.

The M44 Helmet Liner

In 1944 the original 1931 pattern of helmet liner gave way to a new, simpler design. The M44 liner design used felt or felt-like material to affix the leather liner directly to the helmet shell and made use of a web chin strap.

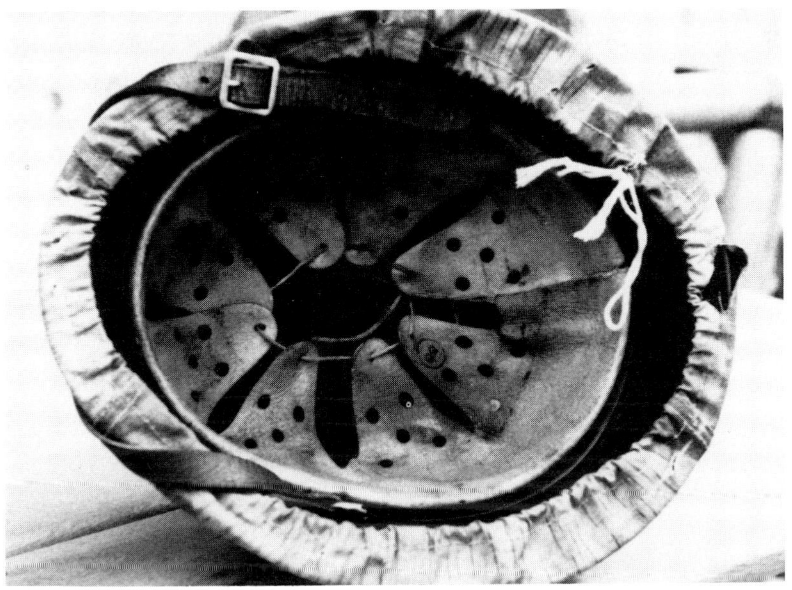

The liner of a **Model 1935**, or **1942 Steel Helmet**. The metal suspension ring is visible as is the **Camouflage Helmet Cover** drawstring.

The Steel Helmet

The Steel Helmet is stamped at the rear with the size of the helmet shell. In some cases information is stamped on the inside of the rim below the split pins. Each of the three split pins is marked on the long tab with the manufacturer's code and date. However unless the helmet is disassembled, a discouraged practice, these will never be seen. The outer aluminum ring is stamped with the manufacturer's name or code and production date plus a size stamp. The leather liner is stamped with the manufacturer's mark or code and production date.

Each foot soldier was issued, and was required to wear, his Identification Disc. The disc contained vital information for identifying the soldier in case of death or an incapacitating wound which would require transport away from the unit.

The Identification Disc was oval and usually made of zinc. It was divided in half by perforated slots, and a cord was threaded through two holes on one side of it.

Items entered on the disc were the personnel roster number, the unit identification and blood group. The personnel roster number, which was also inscribed in the soldier's paybook, was the number assigned to the soldier when he joined the replacement section of his new unit at the recruitment depot. The number of the company and the identification of the unit to which the soldier belonged was also stamped on the front of the disc. The blood-group typing letter identifying the soldier's blood group was stamped either on the front or the back of the disc. This information was mirrored on the other half of the disc. Exact placement of the information depended on the unit's operating procedure.

As an example, one half of an identity disc could look like this:

130

3 / 31 INF REG

A

The 130 was the foot soldier's personnel roster number. The 3 identifies the third company, and the 31 INF REG identifies the Thirty-first Infantry Regiment. The A indicates the soldier's blood group.

The Identification Disc remained unchanged throughout the foot soldier's service. If he were transferred to another unit, only the information in his paybook was altered. However, if a soldier lost the disc, his current unit would replace it with one bearing that unit's identification information and the roster number assigned to the soldier by that present unit.

In case of death, the disc was broken in half. The portion with the cord remained on the soldier's body and the other half was taken, with other personal effects, for future identification and notification of family.

Late War Fabrics and Man-Made Fibers

By 1944 and 1945, war production had reached its height. German industry strived to do more with less or to do the same thing with something else. The use of man-made materials became the standard for production of uniforms and equipment for the foot soldier. Through the use of man-made fibers produced from cellulose, a carbohydrate found in the woody parts of trees, German textile producers reached their highest wartime peak of self-sufficiency.

Germany has forever been known as a land of deep, rich forests. Parts of these forests, rich in heritage of legend and history, fell to provide material for Germany's war industry. The development and use of man-made cellulose fibers for the German military was begun during the 1914-1918 war and continued throughout the interim.

Germany's climate was unsuitable for the production of cotton, and she was therefore required to import and stockpile this precious resource. But German agriculture was able to produce flax and wool. Therefore, the fabric industry could manufacture linen and woolen fabrics. Still, all these natural fibers required growing seasons. The refinements in the manufacture of cellulose-based materials, however, decreased Germany's dependency on these imported and natural fibers.

The cellulose fiber "rayon" is produced by pressing a form of cellulose solution through small holes and then solidifying it into filaments. Rayon is produced in endless filaments varying in size from that of horse hair to that finer than silk; the size of the filament is determined by the diameter of the opening the cellulose solution is forced through.

Two basic types of yarn are produced from this man-made fiber: "rayon" and "spun-rayon." To make "rayon," a number of fiber strands are twisted together and then stretched during production. This produces a strong, shrink resistant yarn for use in fabrics or in the reinforcing web in artificial leather. "Spun-rayon" is produced by drawing the filaments into a straight rope or "tow" and then chopping it into equal lengths. This chopped fiber is called "staple," and it can be spun into artificial cotton, silk, or wool. The German cellulose chemists were able to produce man-made fibers to meet all the needs of the military uniform and equipment manufacturers.

Both "rayon" and "spun-rayon" were used for production of military uniforms and equipment prior to the beginning of the war, as Germany expanded her military. Man-made fibers were blended with natural fibers to produce uniform cloth and equipment webbing. The goal of this use of man-made fibers was to ease the drain on the reserves of cotton, wool and linen. The extension of the war into 1942 saw increased use of man-made fibers.

The Reversible Winter Over-Uniform was the first example of use of a large proportion of man-made fabric. The shell of the over-uniform was made completely of "spun-rayon" yarn in the form of "artificial cotton." The insulating layer of the uniform was a combination of a high percentage of "spun-rayon" yarn, or cellulose wool and a small portion of recycled waste wool. All of the webbing for the securing of the over-uniform was made of "spun-rayon" yarn.

Natural cotton and linen fibers were blended with increasing amounts of, or completely replaced by, man-made "spun-rayon" fibers. The Camouflage Smock, Camouflage Helmet Cover, underclothing, uniform linings, webbing, and drill cloth were produced from "spun-rayon" yarns.

Protective uniform items such as the Reversible Anorak were produced from specially treated "rayon" yarn which provided needed strength, lightness and water repellency.

By the end of 1943, the fiber content of the uniform cloth for the Service Tunic and Trouser began to show the economic strain of the war. Cellulose wool, recycled wool, and non-woolen animal fibers were used by German factories for the production of the uniform cloth. The use of the recycled wool and non-woolen animal fibers accounted for the hard feel and rough appearance of the uniform.

In 1944 recycled wool and non-woolen animal fibers in the uniform fabric was again reduced and replaced by a higher percentage of cellulose wool. The use of more cellulose woolen fibers brought on a visible change in the color of the foot soldier's uniform. The olive color of what became "Fieldgrey 1944" became more apparent in uniforms produced of, or repaired with, material with a high cellulose wool content. This color change was because the fabric dyes reacted with cellulose woolen fabric. By this late period of production, the availability of dyes also caused varied colors in uniform cloth.

"Rayon" yarn threads were used in portions of the production of woven and embroidered uniform insignia from before the war. By 1944 and 1945 all uniform insignia was made from "rayon" yarn. Thread used to sew uniforms together was blended with cotton or was made completely of "spun-rayon" yarn. "Rayon" and "spun-rayon" yarns produced into threads have a soft feel and will not melt when exposed to flame.

The trees of the German nation also provided the basis for the production of "artificial leather." By using wood pulp mixed with chemical binders and laminated over a "rayon" yarn web frame, very durable individual equipment was produced.

No other form of resource was used for production of manmade fabric or thread during the period of the war. German technology for the development of synthetics from non-cellulose sources was available, but these synthetics were developed and used in other directions of war production. Nylon, for example, was never used for production of uniform cloth, thread or insignia. The German war industry had found in the nation's forests all that was required for production of uniforms, insignia, and equipment.

GENERAL FIBER CONTENT OF FABRICS USED FOR THE PRODUCTION OF UNIFORMS, EQUIPMENT AND INSIGNIA BY THE GERMAN ARMY IN 1944-1945

The varying percentage of fiber content in the fabrics used for the production of uniforms, equipment and insignia was controlled by the stocks of raw materials available to the individual factories. Therefore the content of the fabrics was never exactly the same. In general the following table of percentages is correct and when it is used in combination with the color photos, fabric identification will be possible.

WOOLEN UNIFORM CLOTH OF 1942 TO 1943
(color photo 18):
New Wool 30% Cellulose Wool 70%
WOOLEN UNIFORM CLOTH OF 1943
(color photo 2):
Recycled Wool and Non-Woolen Animal Fibers 30%
Cellulose Wool 70% (the amount of Non-Woolen Animal
Fibers mixed with the Recycled Wool was higher in this cloth).
WOOLEN UNIFORM CLOTH OF 1943-45
(color photo 4):
Recycled Wool and Non-Woolen Animal Fibers 10-30%
Cellulose Wool 70-90% (the amount of Non-Woolen Animal
Fibers mixed with the Recycled Wool was lower in this cloth).
UNIFORM LINING CLOTH 1943 TO 1945
(color photo 10):
Artificial Silk 100%
UNIFORM LINING CLOTH 1944 TO 1945
(color photo 14):
Artifical Cotton 100%
CAMOUFLAGE UNIFORM CLOTH 1942 TO 1945
(color photos 8 and 10):
Artificial Cotton 100%
WIND AND WATERPROOF CLOTH 1942 TO 1943
(color photo 6):
Tightly woven Natural Cotton 30%
Rayon Yarn 70%
WIND AND WATERPROOF CLOTH 1943 TO 1945
(color photo 12):
Tightly woven Rayon Yarn 100%
HERRINGBONE TWILL 1943 TO 1945
(color photo 15):
Artificial Cotton and Linen in varying percentages
(by the end of war the Artificial Cotton content was dominant).
UNIFORM INSIGNIA 1943-1945
(color photos 2 and 4):
Artificial Silk and/or Artifical Cotton 100%
WEB EQUIPMENT HARNESS 1943-45
(color photo 21):
Rayon Yarn 100%.

The Fieldgrey Greatcoat with Large Collar

The changes to the Standard-Pattern Fieldgrey Greatcoat with Dark Blue-Green Collar began in 1939 with the abolishment of five of the buttonholes on the right side of the coat. Only one buttonhole was retained on this side. To hold the coat front in place a large horn or plastic button was attached either to a cloth strip or directly to the inside of the coat. In 1940 a fieldgrey cloth collar and slip-on shoulder boards were introduced for use in field service greatcoats. In 1942 the size of the greatcoat collar was nearly doubled to provide greater protection for the foot soldier's neck and head.

The Fieldgrey Greatcoat With Large Collar retained the other appearances of the traditional greatcoat by keeping the twelve fieldgrey pebbled buttons in the double-breasted style, and the half-belt in the rear. By regulation the greatcoat collar was worn closed at the throat with a metal hook and eye or with the two top buttons open to show decorations worn around the neck.

Details of the attached hood and large collar.

The Lined Fieldgrey Greatcoat with Large Collar, Attached Hood and Extra Pockets

Another development in the upgrading of the greatcoat was a version of the Fieldgrey Greatcoat with Large Collar, lined with woolen-blend material for extra warmth, and with an attached hood of woolen-blend material and extra side slash-pockets positioned above the side pockets with flaps.

This later version of the greatcoat was normally produced from late war quality woolen fabric. However, this greatcoat was also produced as a modification of existing earlier patterns of greatcoats. The lining and attached hood were usually of grey, black or fieldgrey blanket-quality woolen-blend material. The additional side slash-pockets were lined with the blanket material instead of linen or artificial silk cloth.

This soldier is wearing the **Lined Greatcoat**. The attached hood is visible at the neck. The large collar is made of late war cloth, the coat itself is made of early war cloth. The soldier has his hands in the extra pockets.

The Animal Fur Lined Fieldgrey Greatcoat

The Animal Fur Lined Greatcoat was as an extreme cold weather uniform accessory. The Animal Fur Lined Greatcoat was issued to sentries, guards and any other foot soldiers who needed extra protection during the performance of their duties.

Versions of the Animal Fur Lined Greatcoat were varied by construction. Normally the coat was lined with sheepskin, but additions of fur collars and leather reinforcing patches gave a varied appearance.

Although the Fieldgrey Greatcoat in any of its versions would have probably been replaced by the newer versions of winter garments in extreme cold field conditions, it never disappeared from the uniform of the foot soldier and was worn until the end of the war in 1945.

The Undergarments

The foot soldier of 1944 and 1945 wore two variations of the basic underclothing. Until 1943 and the introduction of the final pattern of the Issue Shirt, the foot soldier wore the prewar type of underclothing, consisting of a long underwear-style top and bottom. The underwear was made of machine kint cotton-"spun rayon" blend fabric. The prewar issue underwear was uncolored and retained the natural fiber appearance. After the beginning of the war underwear was dyed green for field camouflage.

With the introduction of the Issue Shirt, the collarless, long underwear top was no longer issued to the foot soldier. Due to the requirement that all existing stocks of long undershirts be exhausted, the foot soldiers of any unit could wear a variation of undergarments.

The Knitted Gloves

The Knitted Gloves were also a prewar woolen-blend, cold-weather item. The gloves were issued in four sizes, indicated by the number of white or green colored rings knitted into the grey cuff. The glove was issued to and used by foot soldiers until the end of the conflict in 1945.

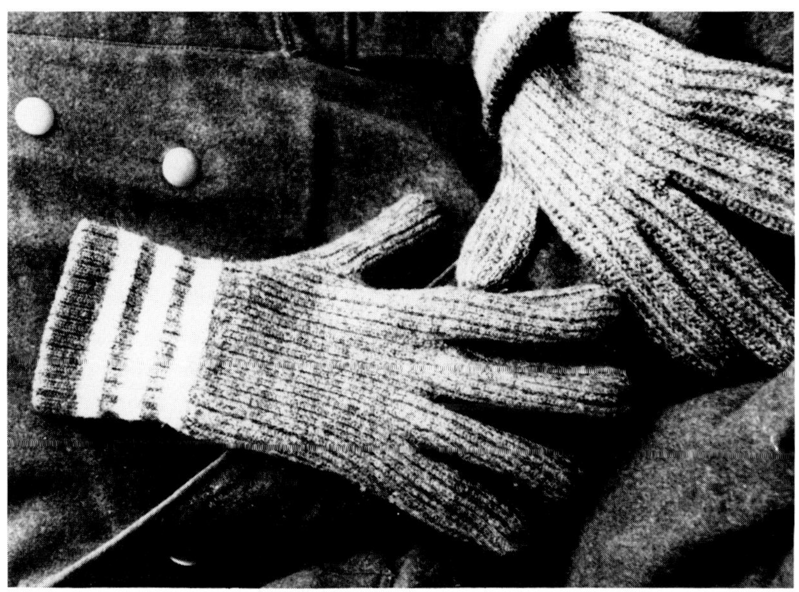

The Model 1942 Sweater

The Model 1942 Sweater was manufactured from grey knitted wool and "spun rayon" yarns. The M42 was of a turtleneck design with snug-fitting cuffs and waist. The sweater was worn under the service tunic and was issued until the end of the war. The sweater was a very popular item with the foot soldier, and it was commonly worn in season.

The Knitted Toque was a prewar-issue, cold-weather item that found continued use throughout the conflict. The toque was a grey, knit tube which was pulled over the head and neck, leaving the face exposed.

The **Knitted Toque** and **Socks**.

The Knitted Socks and Footwraps

The Knitted Sock was made from wool and "spun rayon" yarns. The sock was produced in four sizes, and the size was indicated by a white or green colored ring or rings knitted into the top; the larger the number of rings, the larger the sock.

In 1944 another version of knitted stocking was produced and issued. This sock was a knit tube, closed at one end, without a reinforced heel and designed to fit all sizes of foot.

The Footwrap was also used by the foot soldier to protect his valued feet. The Footwrap was a seamless square of quality woolen or cotton flannel cloth. The art of wrapping the foot was a skill learned with time, and the Footwrap was usually found in the boot of "Der alte Hase."

Other Than Strictly Issue Knitted Items

Many knitted items were supplemented by gifts sent from home. Sweaters, gloves, mittens, ear-warmers, socks, scarves and other items made of high quality natural wool yarn and produced by the hand of a loving mother, wife or sweetheart were worn long and hard. It was not uncommon to find these "home-made" items in favored use on any front.

A foot soldier either learned how to mend his own knitted items or quickly found another foot soldier who could. As cold days approached, a person who could knit and mend knitted items was in great demand.

The Issue Shirt

The German foot soldier in 1944 and 1945 was issued the final design of shirt produced for the Army. The Issue Shirt was made of a finely knitted cotton and "spun-rayon" yarn blend fabric. This long-sleeved shirt was designed so that it could be worn without the service tunic in hot weather. The Issue Shirt had an attached collar, provisions for shoulder boards and two button-down, pleated patch pockets. The shirt was a pullover with a neck opening to the lower chest which closed with four metal, plastic, or pressed paper buttons. The cuff had two buttons to adjust the wrist closure. The sleeves could be worn either down or up when worn in "shirt sleeve order."

When worn with the service tunic, the collar of the Issue Shirt replaceed the tunic collar liner. The shirt could be worn with the collar placed either inside or outside the service tunic collar.

The Quilted Winter Undergarments

To protect the foot soldier from severe cold, quilted undergarments were produced. They were made from a wide assortment of fabrics, but the standard design called for the layering of light weight wool and cellulose wool composite fabric between artificial silk or other artifical fabrics. The undergarment consisted of a coat, wrapped around the body and tied with cloth strips and trousers which also were tied in place with cloth strips.

The Quilted Winter Undergarments were meant to be worn under the service tunic and trouser. This required that the service uniform clothing items be loose fitting, not always the case. As a result, the undergarments were sometimes worn over the service uniform between the Greatcoat or the Winter Over-Uniform. The Quilted Undergarments could also be worn as an outergarment if outergarments were in short supply.

Materials used to make Quilted Winter Undergarments were often donated by German civilians during Winter Relief Campaigns. Undergarments with an interior layer of brightly patterned drapery fabric were not uncommon.

These **Quilted Winter Under Trousers** are being worn as an outer garment.

Pay and Allowances

The lowest ranking German foot soldiers of 1944 and 1945 were generally conscripts or draftees. As a conscript, the foot soldier received the pay and allowances of a non-professional soldier. For a foot soldier with less than two years in the Army, this translated into 30.00 Reich Mark (RM) per month in War Service Pay. If the conscripted foot soldier was married, he received added compensation in the form of Civilian Family Support. The amount of this compensation was determined by the number of dependents the foot soldier claimed. The foot soldier received his War Service Pay from his unit's paymaster. The Civilian Family Support payment was made by the professional armed service officials (civil service) located in the garrison near the foot soldier's home. This payment was usually made by check to the bank account of the soldier's dependent.

Reich Mark 130 and change, a Senior Private's war-time monthly earnings. The notes from top to bottom: **RM 100, RM 20, and RM 5.**

Reich's coinage from top to bottom: **RM 5, RPf 10, RPf 5, and RPf 1.**

Professional soldiers, ones who enlisted into the Army, received War Service Pay and Armed Forces Regular Pay. The Armed Forces Regular Pay included basic peacetime pay, quarters allowance and, if applicable, allowance for dependent children. The Regular Pay for a professional soldier up to the rank of Senior Private First Class was RM 77.50 per month. In combination with the War Service Pay the monthly pay could be up to RM 130.50. In some cases the amount the professional soldier with dependent children received could be less than that received by the conscripted foot soldier with dependent children depending upon the number of children in the family of the conscripted man. The professional soldier received his War Service Pay from his unit's pay master. In order to provide for the professional foot soldier's family, his Regular Pay was deposited into a bank account in his home town.

All foot soldiers serving in a combat area received forty Reich Phennigs (RM .40) per day to help offset the difficult living conditions encountered at the front. This compensation was paid to the soldier by the unit paymaster during each pay period. This front line compensation and the War Service Pay was paid to the foot soldier in advance of his actual service. This payment could be made monthly or at intervals of no less than every ten days. These payments were made free of income-tax deductions.

The allowances for quarters and family, for both conscripted and professional soldiers, were subject to a sliding taxation scale. These allowances were paid into the soldier's bank account, two months in advance of his regular pay, to insure the financial well-being of the soldier's family.

The Gaiter

The Gaiter (legging) was issued to all non-front-line and replacement soldiers from 1940 onwards. The gaiters were made from brown, grey or green heavy cloth reinforced with leather and held in position by two leather straps and buckles. When worn correctly, the male end of the buckle strap faced the rear and the trouser leg was pulled and wrapped tightly forward to prevent undue wear on the trouser material by rubbing against the other leg.

The Gaiter was never widely accepted by those who had worn the "Dice Shaker." From its first appearance the gaiter conjured up images of defeat, mostly because replacement troops wore them as they reached their new front-line units. The old veterans could see how many men were new and how many of the old comrades were gone. This coupled with the stalemates and defeats of the last years of the war compelled the old veterans to call them "retreat gaiters" and "dog blankets."

The Leather Marching Boot

The Leather Marching Boot, or "Dice Shaker," was a traditional symbol of the German foot soldier. The boot was normally issued in black leather and had a boot height that corresponded to the size of the foot. The marching boot was not always manufactured with boot nails. By 1940, the issue of this boot was restricted to front-line units.

By 1944 and 1945 the "Dice Shaker" was a prized item among the German foot soldier because of its high quality leather and symbolic status. The Leather Marching Boot was usually part of the uniform of NCOs or officers who made up the cadre of re-forming units.

The Short Lace-up Ankle Boot

After 1940 the Short Lace-Up Ankle Boot was issued to all Army recruits instead of the traditional marching boot. The boot was issued in both black and natural leather. By 1944 and 1945 the short boot was highly visible among new foot soldiers, who made up the replacement units.

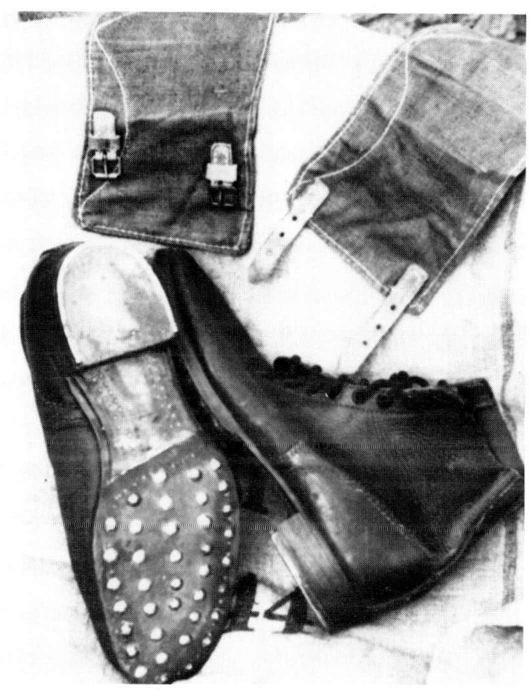

Der alte Hase

Sex and the Foot Soldier

For the German Army soldier on the front lines in 1944 and 1945, women existed only in memory and in photos. For the front line soldier who was fortunate enough to get home leave, or was the recipient of a wound that required convalescent leave, or was a member of a unit that was pulled from the lines for revitalization, the pursuit of the opposite sex again became possible. For many young soldiers having sex was perceived as a final rite of passage into soldierhood.

The sexual desires of the soldier were recognized by the German Army, and in order to ensure that the soldier remained fit for duty, all soldiers were provided the education and the means to prevent the contraction of venereal diseases. Early in their training soldiers were taught about all the aspects of gonorrhea, syphilis, and other venereal disease of the time. Not only was the soldier shown very graphic photos of the results of contracting venereal disease and of the long term consequences of the disease going untreated, but also often afflicted soldiers were shown as living examples.

The soldier received medical support from the unit medical personnel in the prevention of sexually transmitted diseases. Following sex, he could report to the unit medic for treatment with preventative salve and solution. Condoms were produced for the German military and were issued to the soldiers. They were a required item, checked along with uniform and papers, prior to a soldier's release from the garrison on pass. Condoms were required to be carried in the field dressing pouch of the service uniform.

The prevention of pregnancy was not stressed in training; in fact the opposite was true as the government solicited an increased birthrate to bolster the population. By 1944 and 1945, however, the realities of raising a child in a time of great uncertainty caused caution among responsible sex partners.

An issue condom package. The writing on the package indicates that these condoms are for use only by the German military and to destroy after use.

The Huertgen Forest

In September of 1944 the American Army began to attempt the penetration of the Siegfried Line south of Aachen. The area they chose to attack, the Huertgen Forest, was north of where we were to be refitting and resting. With the renewal of the American offensive, we of the 89th Infantry Division were once again placed in the front line.

This private is waiting in the forest. Of interest is the **Camouflage Helmet Cover** made from the "tan-water" or second pattern camouflage cloth.

We had arrived in the North Eifel mountains with about 350 men in our regiment, the 1056th. Our little group, the First Battalion, was composed of members of all our regimental organizations such as our infantry, artillery, engineer and other support troops. Now, after the march from France, we were all infantry! Upon arrival we were refitted with all sorts of replacements. Joining us were new recruits from an armored infantry replacement brigade, some local security police and some troops from a fortress battalion. None of these new arrivals were much to see. We prepared for action by occupying a section of the first defensive line of the West Wall fortification southeast of Monschau near Rohren. Before long there was heavy fighting. This fighting would take our battalion north into the Huertgen Forest. The Huertgen Forest was to be a continuation of the horrors we had faced in the summer.

Watching for signs of enemy activity.

The area of the Huertgen Forest is a place of beauty and of terror. The task one faces in the forest determines how you see it. The forest is composed mainly of tightly packed evergreens with dense and uncleared undergrowth. The forest is divided by small rivers and streams that have cut sharp gorges into the landscape. The forest floor is covered with a deceptive layer of castoff pine needles. Below this layer is rock and a high ground water level.

Unit and town direction signs in the Huertgen Forest.

The forest is cold and wet in the fall and winter. The cold hangs heavy on the ground. As the elevation is high, wet sleet or snow can come quickly. Inside the forest darkness comes very quickly, and the dense forest canopy blocks any light from the moon or stars. Even in the day the forest is dim except for the occasional penetration of a sunbeam. The wind rushes constantly among the branches of the trees and hides the other forest sound.

Through the Huertgen Forest, runs the second defensive line of the West Wall fortifications. These fortifications, built before the war to safeguard Germany's borders, were bolstered in 1944 with earth and wood bunkers. Here, in these bunkers, the forest was not such a bad place. The bunkers were dry, and therefore, warmer than the outside. All the bunkers were situated so as to allow the maximum amount of small arms fire possible to be directed at the enemy without exposing ourselves to their return fire. The bunkers were designed to support and defend one another by interlocking the areas into which the soldiers inside the bunkers could shoot. All of the approaches to the bunkers were heavily mined and blocked with barbed wire. All in all the bunkers were a very good place to be with one exception: the bunkers could not move. Once the Americans found a bunker they were able to make things rather hot for the occupants.

Our infantry training teaches us that the best defense is to attack. In the months that followed, our company attacked all along the southern flank of the battle. Beginning as we did southeast of Monschau, we fought up to the area of Vossenack where we helped pinch off an American advance. The forest helps during the attack by hiding the noise soldiers make when they move. The forest teaches soldiers to be still when the wind stops its rushing through the branches. When the wind stills, the defender's ears are pricked for any sound. The rain which pelts the forest also disguises noise, but it turns the ground into a bog. The rain turns hillside slopes into slick, treacherous nightmare of walking. The rain turns uniform clothing into sodden, chilling burdens. Each step taken in the dark forest is a step into mystery as it is impossible to see, and a light or flame is a call for the Death Angel!

By day the forest protects the soldier from the hunting

"Jabos." To the pilots above, the earth below is a swirling sea of green. The trees cause mortar rounds to explode high in the trees. This also is a blessing or a curse, depending on how you are positioned on the ground. If you are under cover, then this tree detonation is of great value as the round will not dig into your place of safety and explode. If you are exposed, then this tree detonation is a curse, as the fragments fly in all directions from above, tearing the flesh and maiming the body.

The forest can cause the most proficient navigator to question his bearings. No one is ever really sure of where he is in the forest. Without a significant landmark, each tree and the area surrounding it looks the same.

The fighting in the Huertgen Forest showed us that we could stop the Americans when we fought them without their "Jabos" and many tanks. In the German forest, the German infantry soldier was the master of his world. For over four months we proved this again and again to the American divisions sent at us. In December the tables again turned on the Americans. To our south, the Ardennes Offensive brought the Americans a very early Christmas present.

A very serious reminder about light discipline in the Huertgen Forest.

Paperback Pocket Books for Soldiers

Publishing houses in Germany produced copies of new novels and old classics in a lightweight, compact form designed to be sent to the front for the exclusive use of soldiers!

This swashbuckling novel, written in 1944, was printed by the regional Nazi Party publishing house of Bayreuth. Copies of this book were sold through the Field Post Issue Point of Bayreuth. Other books were produced and marketed in the same manner all over Germany and the occupied areas.

The text on the back cover explains that the Bayreuth Field Post Issue Point has provided this book for soldiers. The weight and size are such that it can be sent in a field post package. The buyer is encouraged to not let the book remain in the living room of the home in Germany as the book is meant for the front line soldier. Soldiers are encouraged to share the book with others after they have read it.

Single copies of this book were sold for RM 1.20. The purchase of large orders was encouraged as the price of each copy in such an order was lower.

The Reversible Winter Over-Uniform

The Reversible Winter Over-Uniform was developed after the bitter experience of the winter fighting in Russia during 1941 and 1942. The Over-Uniform provided excellent protection against the extreme cold encountered during the long months of winter combat. The earliest version of this uniform was produced in a mousegrey exterior color that was reversible to white; however, later the standard Army camouflage patterns were used for the exterior. The design was such that the Over-Uniform fitted over the service uniform and personal equipment, with ammunition carried in the pockets for quick access.

The Reversible Over-Uniform was manufactured in three weights. The light suit was fashioned from two layers of artifical cotton fabric (either grey and white or camouflage and white). The medium suit had an additional layer of cellulose wool cloth sandwiched between the outer layers. The heavy suit was manufactured from heavy twill fabric with quilted internal lining. The medium weight was the most widely manufactured and issued.

The Reversible Winter Over-Jacket was double-breasted for maximum wind protection and was secured by metal pebbled buttons painted either fieldgrey or white. A draw strap was sewn into the waist, and a drawstring was placed in the jacket hem to increase protection. There was an attached hood with a drawstring. The jacket sleeves were cut long for warmth and coverage, and two small metal, plastic or pressed-paper buttons on the upper sleeves held colored armbands, for friend-foe identification.

The Reversible Winter Over-Trouser was cut, for use with the Felt-and-Leather Winter Boot, and drawstrings placed in the trouser cuffs and waist insured protection. The Over-Trouser fly was fastened with metal pebbled buttons painted either fieldgrey or white, and the same type of button was used to attach the Over-Trouser suspenders. The suspenders were manufactured from heavy herringbone twill cloth, making use of three re-enforced buttonholes to adjust the fit of the Over-Trouser.

In addition to the jacket and trouser that made up the Over-Uniform, there were also mittens and a separate hood. The mittens were of a "trigger" design, that is with a free index finger incorporated between the thumb and finger portion of the mitten. The hood was tight-fitting and tied around the neck. The lower portions of the hood lay on the shoulders, providing more insulation.

The uniform was of identical cut on both the camouflaged and white sides. The thermal quality of the uniform was not as good as it might have been because cellulose woolen fabric was used extensively in the insulating layer. Also, it soon was obvious that the white side became filthy under combat conditions and could not be laundered in freezing frontline conditions. In spite of these drawbacks, stocks of the Reversible Winter Over-Uniform were never exhausted and it remained in service until the end of the war in 1945.

These soldiers are wearing the **Reversible Winter Over-Uniform**. The trousers worn by the soldier on the right are of the second camouflage pattern. Other details found in Vol. I and Vol. II.

The Non-Reversible Winter Over-Uniform

The Non-Reversible Winter Over-Uniform was produced to supplement, and to eventually replace, the Reversible Winter Over-Uniform. Manufactured in either the mousegrey or camouflage patterned artifical cotton cloth which covered an additional layer of cellulose woolen cloth and lined with grey or blue-grey artificial silk, the Non-Reversible Winter Over-Uniform was identical to the camouflaged side of the earlier Reversible Winter Over-Uniform.

The foot soldier needed the warmth and protection of the Winter Over-Uniform, but he did not always need the snow-

The **Non-Reversible Winter Over-Jacket.** Of interest are the large plastic buttons used on this pattern of uniform.

The **Non-Re-
versible
Separate
Hood** exterior.
Of interest is
the ear
opening which
is covered by
only a light
layer of cloth.

The interior of the **Non-Reversible Separate Hood.**
Of interest is the grey artificial silk lining.

camouflage afforded by the white side of the Reversible Winter Over-Uniform. If the foot soldier required snow-white camouflage, then the Two-Piece Snow Suit or the Single-Piece Snow Overall was worn over the Over-Uniform. This option allowed the soldier to remain inside his warm, dry Over-Uniform while he removed and cleaned or exchanged the soiled white camouflage. In many situations the easily-soiled white side of the Reversible Uniform was not essential.

By 1944 and 1945 the Non-Reversible Uniform in combination with the various camouflage snow suits began to be used more in the newly formed field units. Both new and used Reversible Winter Over-Uniform stocks were still being exhausted so both variations were seen as winter clothing for the German foot soldier until the end of the war.

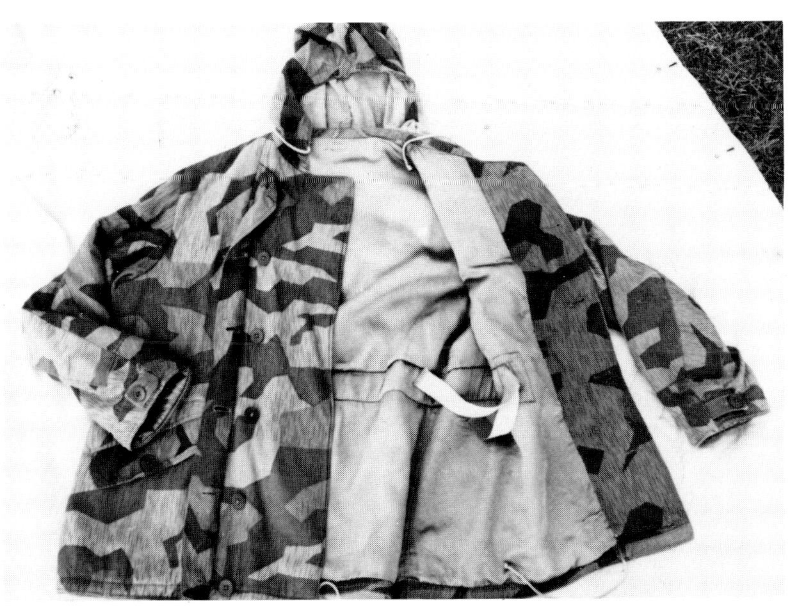

The **Non-Reversible Winter Over-Uniform Jacket.** Of interest is the large web waist drawstrap and the grey artificial silk lining.

The **Non-Reversible Winter Over-Trouser**. Of interest are the plastic buttons and the grey artificial lining.

The rear of the **Non-Reversible Winter Over-Trouser.** Of interest are the web suspenders and adjusting strings.

Camouflage Mix and Match, Use What You Can Get

The Army Reversible and Non-Reversible Over-Uniforms were produced in three outer patterns; mouse-grey, "splinter" camouflage, and "tan-water" camouflage. The Reversible and Non-Reversible style Over-Uniforms were made not only for the Army, but also for the Waffen SS and other paramilitary organizations such as the police. These Over-Uniforms were produced in the camouflage pattern or color of that particular organization. By 1944 and 1945 the supply situation demanded that first priority be placed on providing an Over-Uniform to the foot soldier. The uniformity of the items issued to the soldier

This soldier seems very happy. Perhaps he is determining the compass bearing to the "Goulash Gun." Of interest is the police **Reversible Winter Over-Uniform Jacket** he is wearing.

became unimportant. The uniform parts were issued by size, and mixtures of patterns were common. The front-line foot soldier was far more concerned with having one of each component of the uniform than with color coordination!

The same situation existed in regard to the Camouflage Smock. Not only were Army "splinter" and "tan-water" smocks issued within the same unit, but various patterns of Waffen SS Camouflage Smocks were also worn by the Army foot soldier. Likewise the Camouflage Helmet Cover, if available, would often be mixed within a formation.

Of paramount concern to the front-line German foot soldier in 1944 and 1945 was protection from the harsh elements, a measure of security from sharp enemy eyes and workability.

The Padded Fieldgrey Cloth Three-Finger Mitten

The Padded Fieldgrey Cloth Three-Finger Mitten was provided in order to upgrade the foot soldier's cold-weather uniform. These mittens were manufactured from fieldgrey cloth and lined with woolen blanket material. The mittens could be worn over the issue gloves. The mitten had a leather toggle and loop to hold a pair together and in place on the greatcoat when not in use.

The Padded Fieldgrey Cloth Three-Finger Mitten was also used with other winter clothing items such as the Reversible and Non-Reversible Winter Over-Uniforms.

The Fieldgrey Cloth Ear Protector

The Fieldgrey Cloth Ear Protector was another means of uniform up-grade for the cold weather. The Ear Protector was tied under the chin and completely covered the ears.

The Two-Piece Snow Suit

The Two-Piece Snow Suit was developed to enable the foot soldier to maintain clean, white, winter camouflage clothing while wearing the Reversible Winter Over-Uniform. Later, the Two-Piece Snow Suit would also be worn with the Non-Reversible Winter Over-Uniform, providing camouflage in snow.

The Two-Piece Snow Suit consisted of an over-jacket with an attached hood and an over-trouser. The entire uniform could be laundered in the field and quickly dried, while the soldier kept wearing his warm Over-Uniform.

Note: A photo of the **Two-Piece Snow Suit** can be found in Vol. II.

The Single-Piece Snow Overall

Probably the last snow over-garment variant of the war, the Snow Overall was used in conjunction with the Winter Over-Uniform during the Winter of 1944-45.

The Snow Overall buttoned from the crotch to the neck after being put on in the manner of conventional coveralls. The Snow Overall had an attached hood to provide camouflage for the head and steel helmet. The overall was cut with generous sleeves and provided excellent freedom of movement to the foot soldier wearing it. The cuffs of the legs and arms were adjustable to provide a good fit.

The only drawback to the Single-Piece Snow Overall was the problem encountered if the foot soldier needed to lower his Over-Uniform or Service Trousers. This endeavor required the complete removal of the Snow Overall.

The Felt-and-Leather Winter Boot

The Felt-and-Leather Winter Boot was manufactured in two basic styles. The first style was designed to afford a high degree of mobility while providing warmth and protection to the feet. This style of boot was made with a full felt inner boot, the lower third of which was covered with leather, for strength and waterproofing. The felt edges and boot seams were also reinforced with leather. The boot was issued in both black and brown leather. The fit on the boot top could be adjusted with a buckle and strap. Some leather soles and heels were reinforced with nails or heel plates, and some of the heels were grooved to accept ski bindings.

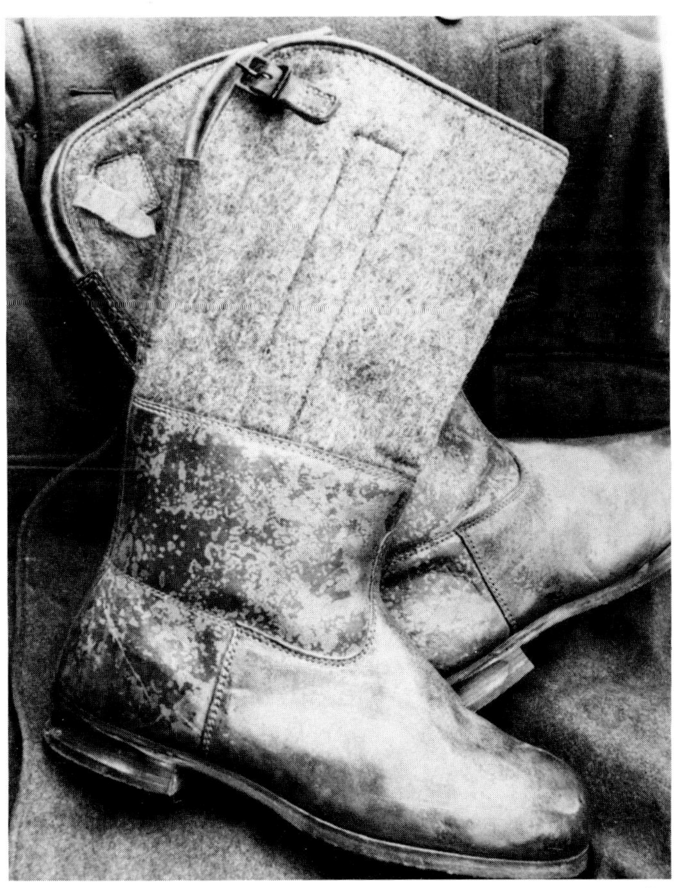

The second style of Felt-and-Leather Winter Boot was an over-boot designed for use by sentries in static positions and provided the maximum insulation and protection possible for the feet. Designed to replace the Woven Straw Over-Boot, this boot was of much heavier construction than the first design. The sole of the boot was wood. The upper portion of the boot was made of thick felt with leather reinforcement. The upper portion had a split down the front which was covered by a leather tongue. This split allowed the foot soldier to put the boot on over his normal footwear. The boot was closed with leather straps and buckles.

The Reversible Windproof Anorak and Trousers

The Windproof Anorak and Trousers were originally issued to mountain troops beginning in 1942, but were soon found in increasing numbers among foot soldiers. The uniform was manufactured from a reversible, windproof "artificial cotton" yarn material. The cloth was white on one side and light brown to grey on the other. The uniform was designed for wear over the service uniform and equipment.

The Windproof Anorak can be easily identified by the three pockets, with flaps, running across the chest. The outermost pockets were pleated, while the center pocket was not. The Anorak also had an attached hood with a lace-up drawstring, and

The **Reversible Windproof Anorak.** Of interest are the three chest pockets and the neck closure.

The rear view of the **Reversible Windproof Anorak**. Of interest are the two hip pockets and the opening for the "tail" which ran from the upper single button, between the legs, to the lower front button. The purpose of the tail was to secure the **Anorak** in winds, but it was seldom used.

the neck was covered with a windproof, button-down flap. The wrists of the Anorak could be secured against wind with tightening straps. A long, tail-like strap at the back could be buttoned between the legs to insure a windproof fit.

The Windproof Trouser was manufactured from the same reversible material as the Anorak. Drawstrings were provided for a secure, windproof fit in the waist and cuffs. The trouser fly was fastened by plastic buttons, and two pockets were sewn into the side seams.

The Windproof Trouser was not as popular with the foot soldier as was the Anorak. The Anorak was commonly worn with the wool service trouser and was worn by the German foot soldier until the end of the war in 1945.

The Camouflage Smock

Common use of camouflage clothing by the foot soldier did not begin until late in the war. Economic, political and logistical factors involved in outfitting the largest service branch with a new camouflage clothing were difficult to overcome. The Army lagged far behind the newer, smaller and more innovative Waffen SS and Luftwaffe Paratroop formations in the development and issue of camouflage clothing.

The Eastern Front winter fighting of 1941 and 1942 emphasized the need for white camouflage; thus the first generation of camouflage clothing for the German foot soldier was born in the

This soldier is wearing a second pattern **Camouflage Smock** with attached hood. Of interest are the neck lace and the waist drawstring.

This soldier is wearing a second pattern **Camouflage Smock** with attached hood and a helmet cover of the same material.

Details of sleeve adjustment strap and button, the side slit pocket opening, and waist drawstring.

Details of the attached hood of the second pattern **Smock.**

Reversible Winter Over-Uniform. With the basic success of the Over-Uniform, the development of other items proceeded. As 1943 wore on, the army began experimentation and issue of other items of camouflage clothing such as the Camouflage Helmet Cover and the Camouflage Smock.

The Waffen SS Camouflage Smock provided the basis for the design of the first Army Camouflage Smock. This smock was of a full, mid-thigh length, pullover design without collar. The sleeve cuffs could be adjusted with cloth straps and buttons. The neck yoke was split to the lower chest and was closed by means of an eye and lace system. The waist was adjusted by tightening a cloth belt which ran through a tunnel sewn to the smock

A first pattern **Camouflage Smock** without hood.

midsection. The Camouflage Smock was worn over the service uniform, and access to the tunic was provided by two vertical slash pockets just above the waistband. The first pattern Camouflage Smock was made from artificial cotton material printed on one side with the Army "Splinter" camouflage pattern.

The second pattern Army Camouflage Smock modified the first design to include a hood intended to replace the Camouflage Helmet Cover. The second pattern smock was produced from artificial cotton fabric printed with the Army "Tan-Water" camouflage pattern.

The Camouflage Smock was intended to be worn over the personal equipment. However, most of the time it was not. When worn under the equipment, the smock skirt was often rolled up and tucked under the Cartridge Belt, exposing the lower portion of the service tunic. Likewise the smock sleeve cuffs were turned back under the wrist adjustment and service tunic cuffs.

The Camouflage Trouser

To complete the camouflaging of the foot soldier, a Camouflage Trouser was designed for use over the service uniform trouser. The Camouflage Trouser was held in place by a waist drawstring and adjustment of the blouse on the boot was made by means of drawstrings in the cuff. The Camouflage Trouser was not widely issued or used by the German foot soldier.

Camouflage Uniforms and Equipment
Field-Made Items

Production of camouflage uniforms and equipment was a mainstay for the regimental tailor or anyone else who could get his hands on camouflage cloth and a way to stitch it up.

For the most part it was officers and sergeants who had the desire plus the resources for custom camouflage uniforms and equipment. Camouflage gear was a status symbol of front line personnel, and in some situations, the camouflage uniform was

This soldier is wearing a field-made M44 pattern camouflage jacket and M43 pattern cap.

not used for concealment from the enemy. This was not always the rule as enemy marksmen were very good at their craft by 1944 and 1945. Field-made camouflage gear was frequently used by combat foot soldiers; this was especially true for snipers.

The most frequent items produced were tunics and trousers. The tunics were usually cut along the lines of regulation service tunics because this was what the tailor knew and had patterns for. Camouflage tunics were made with or without linings, depending on the foot soldier's need and the tailor's allotted

Field-made camouflage trousers.

working time and charge. Pockets were always a key factor in the production of a camouflage tunic, as foot soldiers wanted pockets on the inside and out for carrying valuables.

There was no real rule about putting rank, branch, or national insignia on a camouflage tunic as they were not authorized by regulation and therefore fell under the whim of unit commanders. Official camouflage rank insignia was rarely encountered.

This NCO has a field-made M36 pattern jacket.

Trousers were produced in the style of the service trouser with the possible addition of extra pockets on the leg such as seen on HBT tank uniforms. Again, quality depended on time and the charge.

Other popular items were caps, face masks, gloves, mittens, Waffen SS-style smocks, helmet covers and rucksacks. These items were made to the specifications of the individual foot soldier and therefore had no exact design. The normal material used in the manufacture of field camouflage uniforms and equipment was the Shelter Quarter in the first or "Splinter" camouflage pattern. Items were also made from "liberated" material such as Italian camouflage fabric. Uniforms and equipment were fastened with standard metal, plastic, or horn buttons. Zippers were also used when they could be found and afforded. Other regulation uniform and equipment hardware was used as required.

The Equipment

This "alte" finds humor in the darkest of situations.

The Cartridge-Belt and Buckle

The Cartridge-Belt and Buckle bearing the inscription GOTT MIT UNS (God With Us) was a symbol of the German Army.

The Cartridge-Belt and Buckle was worn alone or with varying amounts of equipment hung on it. The belt was worn either over the Service Tunic, or in the belt loops provided on the various styles of service trousers.

When the Cartridge-Belt was worn with the M43 Service Tunic, it was held in place by four metal hooks attached to the inside of the tunic. When the Cartridge-Belt was worn with the M44 Service Tunic, it was held in place by two metal suspension hooks. This support system was sufficient for light duty. However, increased combat loads required the use of the Cartridge-Belt Suspenders.

Cartridge-Belts were issued in varying sizes. Adjustment to individual size of the belt could be made by moving the buckle along an adjustment strap sewn onto the back of the Belt.

The early versions of the Cartridge-Belt were made from leather. As the war progressed to the tropical theaters, a web version was developed. By 1944 and 1945, the tropical style web belt was finding wide distribution in the European Theatre of action.

The Cartridge-Belt Buckle, made of pebbled aluminum, began to be replaced by buckles made from steel. These steel buckles were painted field-grey. As the war progressed, aluminum metal became required for other more important war production needs. By 1944 and 1945 the buckle was being produced not only in stamped steel, but in cast "pot metal" and bakelite plastics. The metal versions were painted in varying shades of fieldgrey to darkgreen. The leather or web pouch support tab, long a part of the buckle design, was deleted in the mid-war period.

Here a soldier wears the **Cartridge-Belt** and **Buckle** in shirt sleeve order.

The Cartridge-Belt

The Cartridge-Belt is stamped with the manufacturer's mark or code and date or the RB Nr. on the short tab of leather turned back to make the loop which, when sewn together, holds the metal fitting which hooks into the buckle. Web Cartridge-Belts are ink stamped with the same information in the identical place. It is not unusual for these stamps to be worn off as they are on the inside and constantly rub against the service uniform.

The reverse sides of the two **Cartridge-Belt Buckles**. The leather pouch support tab is found on one example.

The Cartridge-Belt Buckle

If the Cartridge-Belt Buckle is equipped with the sewn on leather tab, the manufacturer and production date or RB Nr. are stamped here. In some cases cast buckles have manufacturer's codes and dates cast into the buckle. Some steel buckles have this same information stamped on the outside edge near the fitting for the hook on the belt. In other cases, genuine buckles have no stamps at all.

MP40 ammunition was carried in cloth and leather pouches. Each pouch held three magazines, each of which held thirty-two rounds of 9mm ammunition. The pouches also held the magazine loading tool. The pouch was attached to the Cartridge Belt by means of two loops sewn to the rear of the pouch. A ring was provided at the top of the pouch for attachment to the Cartridge Belt Suspenders.

In the event that only one ammunition pouch was to be carried, a leather or web loop with an attached metal ring was worn on the Cartridge Belt to provide an attachment point for the Cartridge Belt Suspenders.

An **MP40 Magazine Pouch** with magazines and loading tool.

The Cartridge Pouch for the Kar.98K Rifle

Ammunition for the Kar.98K Rifle was carried in black leather Cartridge Pouches. Each Pouch was divided into three pockets, which were sub-divided into two sections. Each section would hold a five-round stripper clip of 7.92 mm rifle ammunition, with each pouch containing thirty rounds.

On the rear of each pouch, a metal suspension ring was located for connecting the Cartridge Belt Suspenders. The Pouch was affixed to the Cartridge Belt by two leather loops which were sewn and riveted to the rear of the Pouch.

Ammunition for the G41 Semiautomatic Rifle was carried in these same pouches.

Lernen durch Erfahrung

G43/K43, MP38/40, MP43/MP44/STG44, Cloth Magazine Pouches

The manufacturer's mark or code and the date of production is ink-stamped in black or purple on all cloth magazine pouches. On leather-bound pouches, the nomenclature, i.e. MP44, MP38/40, etc. is stamped into one leather belt loop while the manufacturer's mark of code and date of production is stamped into the other. The RB Nr. can take the place of the date and manufacturer in some cases.

The Magazine Pouch for the Model 43 Semiautomatic Rifle (G43)

The 7.92mm G43 Semiautomatic Rifle was loaded with ten-round box magazines. The pouch designed to hold these magazines was a two-section container produced from either leather or cloth. Loops made of variations of these same materials were used to attach the pouch to the Cartridge Belt. A metal ring was provided on the back to secure the pouch to the Cartridge Belt Suspender. In normal use one G43 Magazine Pouch could be worn in conjunction with a Kar.98K Cartridge Pouch.

The **Magazine Pouch** for the G43. This soldier has acquired another pouch and set of magazines.

The Magazine Pouches for the Machine Pistol 43, Assault Rifle 44

The 7.92mm "Short" ammunition used in the thirty-round magazines of the MP43/StG44 was carried in a three-compartment magazine pouch. Each foot soldier equipped with the MP43/StG44 was issued a pair of these pouches. Besides holding six magazines, the pouches contained the loading tool and spare weapons' parts. The MP43/StG44 pouches were produced from cloth with the early production versions being reinforced with leather. The pouches were attached to the Cartridge Belt by means of loops sewn to the rear of the pouch. A ring attachment was provided to fasten the MP43/StG44 pouches to the Cartridge Belt Suspenders.

The **Magazine Pouch** for the MP43/StG44.

The Cartridge-Belt Suspenders

The Cartridge-Belt Suspenders were used to support the weight of the individual equipment attached to the Cartridge-Belt, and to provide pack straps for the Combat Assault Pack, the Model 1939 Field Pack, or the Canvas Rucksack.

The Cartridge-Belt Suspenders were of two basic styles: the dismounted and mounted. The foot soldier would normally be issued the heavier dismounted style, identified by a wider shoulder strap, heavier construction, D-ring attachments on the rear

This soldier is wearing **Cartridge-Belt Suspenders**. Of interest is the **Machine Gun Accessory Pouch** and the D-ring Belt Support that is being worn in place of a pouch.

of the shoulder harness, and attached lower pack straps used for securing the bottom of any attached pack.

The Cartridge-Belt Suspenders issued to the foot soldier of 1944 and 1945 were produced in web, leather or artificial leather. The fixtures of the Cartridge Support Suspenders were steel. The web version of the Cartridge-Belt Suspenders made use of friction-style strap adjusting devices instead of the pronged-buckle devices found on the leather or artificial leather versions.

The rear section of the **Cartridge-Belt Suspenders**. Of interest are the D-ring attachment points on the shoulders.

The Cartridge-Belt Suspenders

The Cartridge-Belt Suspenders are stamped with the manufacturer's mark or code and date or RB Nr., in one of two locations: on the inside of the shoulder straps and the D-ring or on the outside of the disc of leather sewed under the ring where all three straps meet. Web Cartridge-Belt Suspenders are ink-stamped with the same information on the straps. While not common, leather suspenders with ink stamps, which disappeared under any kind of cleaning, were produced.

This corporal is returning his bayonet to its scabbard, perhaps after close combat. He is wearing web **Cartridge-Belt Suspenders.**

Field Post - The Vital Link with Home

Mail from home was of paramount importance in maintaining good morale among German foot soldiers. The Army Field Postmaster provided special stamps for sending airmail and packages to the soldier at the front. These stamps were issued to the soldier at company level by his First Sergeant or Platoon Sergeant.

For the foot soldier fighting at the front in continental Europe there were four basic kinds of field postage stamps issued during the course of the war, two of these initiated in 1944.

The Field Post Airmail Stamp was first issued on 20 April 1940. This stamp shows a flying Junkers Ju-52 transport aircraft bordered on the top by LUFTFELDPOST and on the bottom by DEUTSCHES REICH printed in cornflower blue on white. The airmail stamp was used by soldiers in distant areas such as Russia, the Balkans or Scandinavia. The soldier at the front was issued four of these stamps per month. The soldier would send two letters home with airmail post and by including a stamp inside these letters, he could receive two replies from home via airmail. Each letter required one stamp until May of 1943, when two per letter were required. At this point the issue to the soldier was increased to eight stamps per month.

The Field Post Package Stamp was first issued on 10 July 1942. The package stamp was red-brown with a typical national eagle circled with ZULASSUNGSMARKE and DEUTSCHE FELDPOST. The corners were marked with German style postal horns. The soldier was issued one stamp per month until 1 September 1942, when the issue increased to two stamps. This issue remained the same until the fall of 1944. With this stamp, a package of up to 250 grams could be sent free to the soldier. Packages weighing 250-1000 grams required the addition of a twenty Pfennig stamp. On 1 September 1942, the weight allowance was increased to 2000 grams, and the package required two Field Post Package Stamps and a forty Pfennig stamp. In the fall of 1944 the package weight limit was reduced to 100 grams because of transport problems.

The Christmas Field Post Package Stamp was first issued on 20 October 1944. This stamp was for Christmas packages of up to 1000 grams sent from home to the front. This Christmas stamp was identical to the First Field Post Package Stamp except for its light green color and smaller size. Soldiers in the Kurland Pocket cut this stamp in half and used it for a Field Post Airmail Stamp.

The final stamp issued was the Two Kilogram Package Stamp. Issued on 24 November 1944, this stamp was a purple-red forty Pfennig stamp with the profile of Adolf Hitler. The word FIELDPOST was printed across the top and 2 Kg printed across the bottom of the stamp in black ink. This stamp was to be used for sending two kilograms of winter clothing to the soldier at the front.

Regular letter size mail to and from the front was sent without postage but marked "Fieldpost." Any mail weighing

Field Post Stamps. Top row: **Field Post Airmail Stamps;** middle row: Christmas 1944 **Field Post Package Stamp** and the 1942-November 1944 **Field Post Package Stamp;** bottom row: The 40RPf. stamp for additional package weight and the final **Two Kilogram Package Stamp.**

more than 35 grams required extra paid postage. Special Feldpost stationery was available to ensure that the weight limit was not exceeded.

The German foot soldier of 1944 and 1945 did not receive mail on any regular basis. The extremely fluid situation of the combat frontlines required that letters be repeatedly rerouted. Mail often arrived in bunches spanning weeks or months of time. Typical of all mail to soldiers in time of war, there were often letters that broke the heart and spirit with news of broken relationships and tragic death or injury.

Mail from home and a loved one was savored not only by the receiver, but also by all of his closest comrades. The smallest detail of "home" in each letter was cherished by all, each one imagining what might be taking place in his own home. The written joys and the sadness were shared by all in the squad.

The Field Post Airmail Stamps allowed the soldier to get some of his mail in short order. The Field Post Package Stamps provided the foot soldier with a way to get special things from home such as photos, small edibles and homemade knitted items. The German civil and military postal systems strove to meet this vital need of the German Army foot soldier.

The Bayonet

The short, final-pattern version of the 84/98 Mauser Bayonet was the standard issue for the foot soldier in 1944 and 1945. This style of bayonet had seen service in 1915 as the Mounted Bayonet. Just prior to the outbreak of the Second World War, bakelite plastic was introduced to replace the wood in the handle grips. By 1944, the bayonet returned full circle to handle grips made of wood.

Had the conflict lasted longer the bayonet might well have fallen into disuse in its original role as part of the foot soldier's equipment. The 1945 modified version of the Kar.98K rifle had no bayonet lug provided in its design. No other standard German Army weapons system developed during the time of the conflict had a bayonet lug designed into its specifications either.

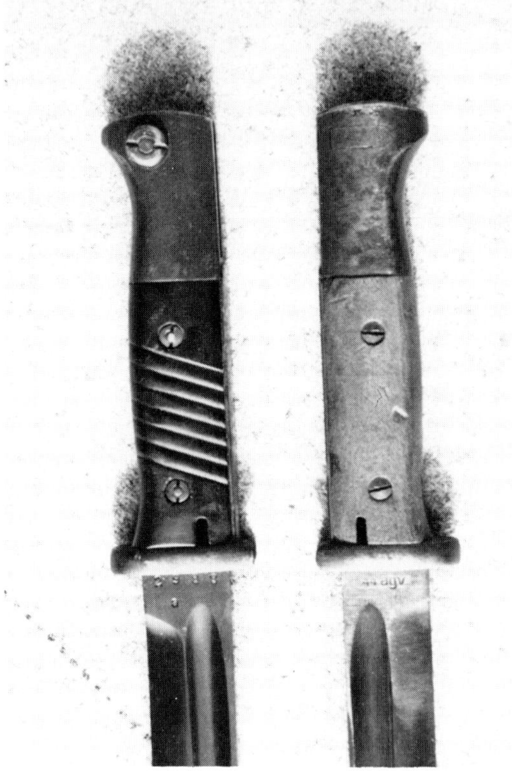

The wooden and the bakelite plastic hand grips of the **Bayonet** are shown here.

The Bayonet and Scabbard

The Bayonet is stamped in front of the hand-guard on the blade, one side with the manufacturer's code and date, the other side with the serial number. The Scabbard is stamped on the throat with the same information.

The Bayonet Frog

The Bayonet was suspended from the Cartridge-Belt in a leather or cotton web hanger known as the Bayonet Frog. The Bayonet and Frog were suspended on the left hip, on top of the Non-Folding Entrenching Tool and Carrier, or just to the front of the Folding Entrenching Tool and Carrier.

Bayonet Frogs were produced in two styles: mounted and dismounted. The mounted style had a narrow leather or web retaining strap to keep the grip of the bayonet from swinging.

Provisions were made after the beginning of the war for all bayonet frogs to be modified into the mounted style; however, this was never completely accomplished and later war production web versions had no retaining strap by design.

For the foot soldier in the European Theatre of the conflict, the standard issue Bayonet Frog was the leather version. The web version was first designed and produced for the African Campaign, but by 1944 and 1945 this pattern was being issued to foot soldiers on the continental fronts.

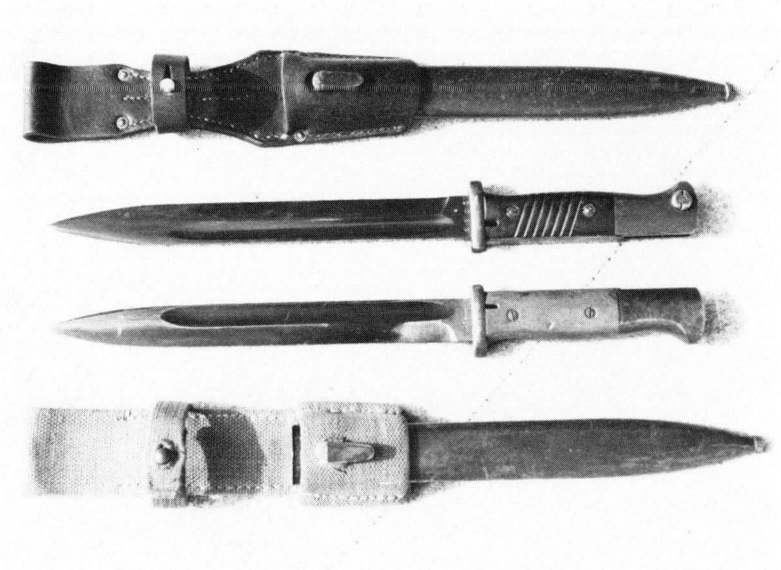

Examples of both leather and web **Bayonet Frogs** with scabbards.

The Bayonet Frog

The Bayonet Frog is stamped on the back side with the manufacturer's mark or code and date or RB Nr. Web Bayonet Frogs are ink-stamped with this information in the same area.

The **Bread Bag** is shown in its correct position. The **Canteen** shown is of interest in that the cup is of orange bakelite plastic.

The Bread Bag

The Bread Bag was an olive-drab colored, water repellent canvas satchel. The Bread Bag was used for carrying a soldier's rations and small items: the fat container, the fork-spoon, the tablet-fuel stove, the individual weapon cleaning kit, the field cap, dust goggles, extra matches, tobacco, playing cards or anything else that would not fit into the Service Tunic pockets.

The outside of the Bread Bag flap could be used as a place to secure the Canteen and the Mess Kit. The Bread Bag was attached to the Cartridge-Belt by means of two button-down loops and a cloth strap with a metal hook, which fit over the top of the Belt. In 1944, a new version was produced that had the button-down portions of the loops sewn into the seam and the hooked center strap replaced with another cloth loop. This version also had an extra pocket sewn on to contain a weapons cleaning kit. The Bread Bag could also be carried slung on a General-Purpose Strap, sometimes called the "Bread Bag Strap."

Lernen durch Erfahrung
The Bread Bag

The Bread Bag is ink stamped with the manufacturer and date on the inside of the flap or, in some cases on the middle cloth belt strap, the one with the metal hook. Later bags may be stamped with an RB Nr. on one of the three leather straps under the flap, usually the long center one.

Lernen durch Erfahrung
The Fat Container

The Fat Container was molded from bakelite plastic and the manufacturer's number code and date are imprinted during the molding process. Both the inside of the lid and the outside of the bottom are marked. The manufacturer's code and the date are separate imprints.

Each foot soldier in 1944 and 1945 received a Fat Container as part of his personal equipment issue. The Fat Container was produced in tan, black, orange and varying shades of white Bakelite plastic. The container was made in two pieces which would screw together.

Part of a foot soldier's daily ration was fat such as butter, margarine, or lard. These fats were normally spread on the bread ration.

One of the lard-based bread spreads, and a great favorite of the foot soldier, was "Schmalz." Schmalz was a great morale builder on any cold morning, and it could easily be made by any foot soldier.

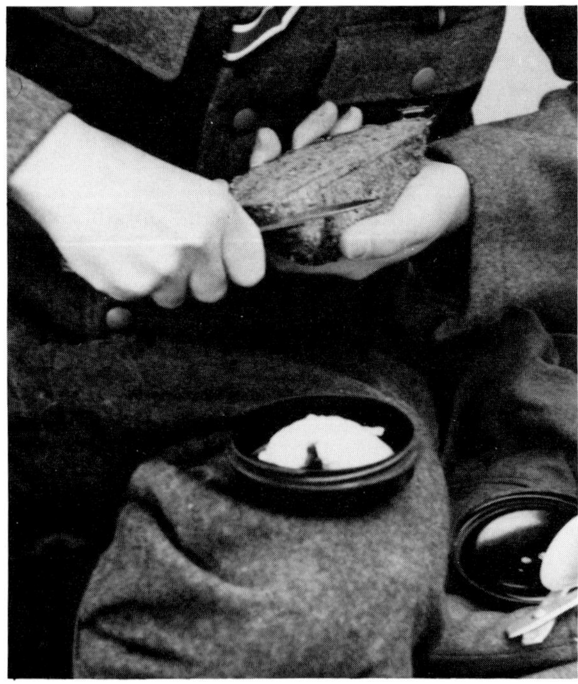

A soldier is having bread with margarine. The margarine ration was kept in the **Fat Container.**

The Mess Kit

The Mess Kit issued to the foot soldier in 1944 and 1945 was constructed of two pieces of painted aluminum or steel, which were designed to fit tightly together to form a single container. The lower "bail" portion was used for soups and stews, while the upper "plate" portion was used for more solid fare. Both pieces could be used for cooking; however, this quickly destroyed the olive-drab or fieldgrey painted finish.

The mess kit sections, when clamped together, could be used to transport rations for future consumption. The mess kit could be strapped to the bread bag, strapped to the combat assault pack, or placed in the mess-kit pouch of any rucksack.

The Mess Kit

The Mess Kit is stamped with the manufacturer's code and date on the "plate" portion, on the riveted fitting to which the handle is hinged, on the "bail" portion, and on one or both of the fittings that hold the wire handle.

Filling the Mess Kit - Pea Soup

The Army canned pea soup is not bad if fixed up properly, but fresh soup made from green or yellow dried peas is always the best bet for pleasing the foot soldier! The best thing about this basic recipe is that you can add to it or take away as the situation fits. Remember, you have to plan ahead with this job as the peas have to soak awhile.

To make pea soup for a squad this is what you need to gather together. Get a small skillet and a pot with a lid that will hold four liters of water. This is no problem if you're working at the "goulash gun." Get a half pound of dried peas, at least two liters of clean water, three mess-kit spoons of butter or fat, a small onion, any other soup vegetables you can get, three mess-kit spoons of flour (this you're going to have to get from the baker), salt, pepper, and if possible a little vinegar.

Into the pot, put the half pound of dried peas, cover them with the water and set them some place safe to soak. If you do this before you go to sleep, they will be ready for use the next day.

Take the peas you have soaked overnight, and put them in a container. Save the water that they were soaking in as it is good for the taste and nobody will have to fetch extra from the water point. Back into the pot, measure two liters of water that has been salted to taste, about one-quarter to one-half of the basic daily salt ration for one man. Use the soaking water and add a bit more if necessary to make two liters. Now add the soaked peas. If you have anything else of good taste from the vegetable world lying about such as carrots, leeks, parsnips, celery or the like, you can chop this up and put it in. Put it on the fire and boil the whole thing. After it has reached the boiling point, remove the pot from the direct heat so that it just simmers. Cover the pot and let it simmer for two hours. Keep watch on this to ensure regularity of the heat and to prevent pilfering!

When two hours is about up, get out the skillet and heat it up. Melt the three spoons of butter or fat and cook the onion until it gets clear; don't burn it. Take the three spoons of flour and mix it with the butter and onion. Cook this until it gets the color of cocoa and take it off the fire. Now take the cooked peas and smash them up as best you can. Next take some of the cooked peas and mix them well with the butter-onion-flour. Keep this up till the skillet is full. Now put the concoction from the skillet back into the pot and mix everything together thoroughly. Put the pot back on the fire and cook for twenty minutes more. Add salt and pepper till it tastes right. If you get your hands on some vinegar, this tastes good in the soup. Again, add till it tastes good.

Other things can be added such as ham, bacon or wurst. Garlic can be added in with the butter-onion-flour mix. This recipe also works with white beans and lentils. Serve Pea Soup with the bread ration and enjoy!

The Canteen and Cup

The Canteen issued to the German foot soldier in 1944 and 1945 was of the same basic design as that at the war's beginning. The Canteen held about a quart of liquid. Early war production models had bodies made of aluminum with a felt cover. The stamped steel or aluminum drinking cup and cap were held in place by a leather strap.

In the early 40s, a version made of compressed-impregnated wood was produced. This wood version was issued with and without the felt cover. Web straps were added to this and the earlier design for use in the tropical campaigns. The cup for this canteen was made of aluminum, stamped steel or bakelite plastic.

In the later period of the war, a canteen was produced from enameled steel. This version was normally covered with felt and had straps made of artificial leather. The cup was of either stamped steel or bakelite construction.

The Canteen was fastened to the D-ring on the Bread Bag by means of a metal spring-clip. For added security, a strap was run from the Canteen neck through a leather loop on the Bread Bag and fitted onto a press fit point on the Canteen bottom.

This **Canteen Cup** is of interest because of its 1944 production date stamp seen between the handles. The **Cup** is resting on an "Esbit" Ration Heater. Complete canteens can be seen in other photos.

The Canteen and Cup

The Canteen is stamped with the manufacturer's mark or code and date of production on the mouth under the cap thread fitting. Additional stamps are located on the Canteen and Cup as follows: On the cup between the handles or on one of the strap fittings on the tapered metal cups, molded into the base on the later bakelite cups, on the harness strap assembly, either stamped or inked onto the strap which held the cap, on the top of the metal cnateen cap, molded into <u>some</u> bakelite caps and on the felt cover on the flap of cloth that protects the back side of the male fittings from rubbing against the flask body. Ideally, all the stamps will be the same.

Our Daily Bread

Tuesday 12 December 1944 The South Eifel Mountains

Soldiers have too many complaints! Everyday I hear their complaints! Not enough of this, not enough of that! What am I talking about?! Why I'm talking about preparing food for hungry soldiers! I'm the master goulash gunner; I'm a cook!

I have only one problem that affects my job; that problem is the war! In 1941 and 1942 all the farmers were in the fields and I got all I could want from the depot. Now, the farmers are on the frontline and, well, you know about water out of a stone! I don't cheat them and I'm not fat! But to hear them tell it, I get every man's breakfast!

This is an example of what each foot soldier is supposed to get every day he is in combat or recovering from it like he is now.

Bread, full grain	(1/2-3/4 of a loaf)
Meats	(1/2 a wurst)
Soy bean flour	(2 tablespoons)
Fish	(one six-inch dried fish)
Vegetables or fruit	(one medium apple)
Potatoes	(three small potatoes)
Legumes	(1/2 cup beans)
Pudding powder	(1/3 cup tapioca)
Condensed skim milk	(1 ounce)
Salt	(2 tablespoons)
Other seasonings	(1 teaspoon pepper)
Spices	(1/3 teaspoon cinnamon)
Fats and bread spreads	(2/3 of a 1/4 pound stick of butter)
Coffee	(1/2 cup of grounds (fine))
Sugar	(4 tablespoons)

I can't always get the authorized classes of ration items, so I have to try to make up the total amounts with foodstuffs of the same type. For example, if all I can get is legumes, then I must make up the vegetable and potatoe ration items with legumes. Nowadays it is tough enough getting anything from the depot and I have to account for every bit of it or I get it in the neck from the old man. My driver spends most of the day looking for things to "requisition."

The soldiers are lucky we are now in a quiet sector for the winter. All the soldiers have to do is watch the Americans watch us, so they can look for wild game. A troop carrier driver bagged a wild pig yesterday and brought it to me to prepare for his platoon; totally secret you know! They'll love my wild pig roast! It's only two weeks to Christmas and I hope the boys have some more good hunting! Perhaps a Christmas goose.

(Standard units of measure and example foods have been added by the author for clarification)

This soldier is holding both the folding and non-folding spades.

The Entrenching Tool

The Entrenching Tool was manufactured in two versions: the non-folding spade and the folding spade. The non-folding spade was of the design from the First World War and was used by German foot soldiers until the end of the Second World War in 1945. Use of captured stocks of non-folding spades was common as the designs were nearly the same. An example of this was the use of Austrian and Polish spades.

The folding spade was designed as a replacement for the older model and began to appear on the belts of the foot soldier in the early 1940s. The folding spade had a pointed front and could be adjusted by means of a bakelite nut to open at a ninety or one hundred-eighty degree angle to facilitate the foot soldier's constant task, digging in.

Both versions were carried in carriers suspended from the Cartridge-Belt on the left hip. Varying versions of the carriers for both styles of spades existed and were produced until the end of the war. Carriers were of varied constructions; produced from leather or metal with leather straps.

This is a non-folding spade in a late war pattern carrier dated 1944. The carrier body is stamped metal and the strapping is leather.

The German foot soldier often relied on his Entrenching Tool for a close-combat weapon. When sharpened to an ax-like edge, the spade became a lethal instrument and could kill with ease. When faced with an impending assault, the foot soldier made sure his Entrenching Tool, no matter which style, was very handy.

This is a first pattern folding spade carrier. The **Bayonet** is held to the carrier by means of a leather loop which can be seen just at the bottom of the **Bayonet Frog.**

Lernen durch Erfahrung
The Entrenching Tool

The Entrenching Tool is stamped on the inside of the blade with the manufacturer's code and date of production and in some cases with a "waffenamt." The non-folding carrier is stamped on the front or back, in between the belt loops. Sometimes there is an ink stamp on the retaining strap. The folding carrier is stamped between the belt loops on the back side.

The Shelter Quarter

In 1944 and 1945 the Shelter Quarter remained an essential item of equipment of the German foot soldier. The Shelter Quarter or Ground Sheet was a piece of strong, light weight fabric cut in the shape of an isosceles triangle. The Shelter Quarter was six feet, three inches on its sides and eight feet, three inches on its base. The tightly woven, water resistant cloth used in the construction of the Shelter Quarter was printed on both sides with the Army "splinter" camouflage pattern. One side was printed in dark shades and the other side in lighter shades in order to blend with any season or time of day.

This soldier is wearing the **Shelter Quarter** as a rain-proof cape.

The Shelter Quarter's main function was as a rain-proof cape or poncho. A flapped hole in the center allowed the head to be thrust through. The use of sixty-two buttons and thirty buttonholes in varying combinations allowed the wearer to adapt the Shelter Quarter to various modes of wear. Each combination allowed maximum movement for a given task. The Shelter Quarter could be fitted for marching, horse-back or cycle riding.

The Shelter Quarter was also used for the construction of a tent. Four Shelter Quarters could be used to create a pyramidal four-man tent, and with the use of additional Shelter Quarters, eight- and sixteen-man tents could be constructed.

The details of the metal gromets used when the **Shelter Quarter** served as a tent. The metal "dish" buttons used for closing the **Shelter Quarter** are also visible.

The Shelter Quarter could also provide a good source of camouflage, when used as a body wrap, and was probably the most widely used camouflage item in the entire German Army. Even in 1944 and 1945 the Shelter Quarter was widely used for this purpose when camouflage pullovers were not available. When the Shelter Quarter was used as a camouflage wrap, the field equipment was normally worn over the outside of the Shelter Quarter.

Material from Shelter Quarters was extensively used to produce camouflage garments. Many different styles of caps, jackets, trousers and other items were manufactured by unit or local tailors to fit the need of the German foot soldier in the closing years of the war.

Lernen durch Erfahrung
The Shelter Quarter

The Shelter Quarter is usually marked on the light side with a purple or black ink stamp which indicates the manufacturer and date of production or RB Nr. The stamp is usually located about six inches inboard of one of the two forty-five degree corners. However, there are occasions when it is found on the ninety degree corner.

Tent Pole, Pins and Rope

Along with the Shelter Quarter, each foot soldier was issued one metal reinforced wooden tent pole, two light metal or bakelite tent pins and one tent rope. This arrangement allowed four foot soldiers to construct one full tent or two foot soldiers to construct a half tent.

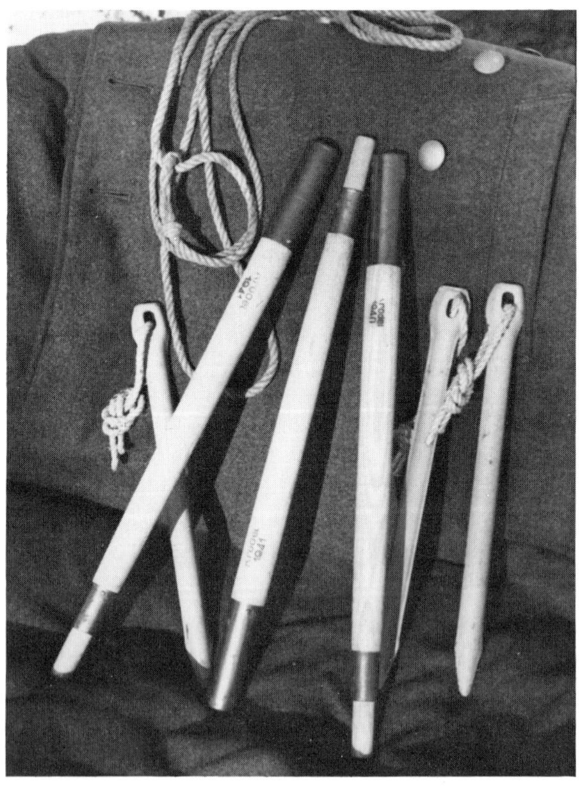

The items necessary to make a one-man shelter from a Shelter Quarter.

What a Difference a Spare Tent Pin Can Make

Finding spare tent poles, pins and ropes at the front was never difficult. Finding one spare tent pin and two spare tent poles provided the foot soldier with a nice option. If the foot soldier found himself alone in the rain and with an option to provide himself shelter, this spare pin and poles allowed him the means. By using the spare pin to fasten down his tent rope, which was attached to the three tent poles supporting the front peak, and his two issue pins to hold down the rear base, the foot soldier's Shelter Quarter became a small but dry shelter.

The addition of a second Shelter Quarter to his equipment provided the single foot soldier with the option of envelope shelter that kept off the rain and cut the wind. A second Shelter Quarter allowed the foot soldier to place a waterproof covering over the reinforced shelter portion of his strongpoint position and still to have one Shelter Quarter for normal use and ac-countability. The German foot soldier of 1944-1945 needed to use all his wits and training to not only survive, but to make a hard life a bit better for himself and his comrades. Getting his hands on a few spare pieces of equipment, like a tent pin and poles, helped meet this end.

1. The **M43 Service Tunic**, **Panzerfaust 60M** and **MP43/StG44** Magazine Pouches.

2. The **Woolen Uniform Cloth of 1943** and the woven **National Insignia**.

3. The **M44 Field Service Tunic, Web Cartridge Belt, Web Suspenders, and G/K43**

4. The **Woolen Uniform Cloth of 1943-45, Web Equipment Harness,** and **National Insignia** embroidered in artificial silk on artificial cotton. This was the final pattern produced from late 1944 till 1945.

5. The **Reversible Windproof Anorak.**

6. Wind and waterproof cloth of 1942-45 as used in the **Anorak.** Both the dark tan and white sides of the **Anorak** are shown.

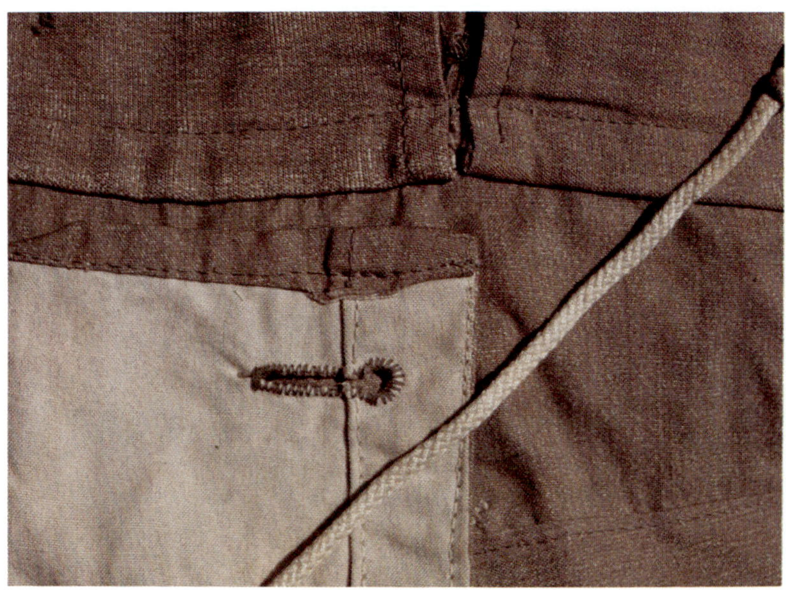

7. The second pattern **Camouflage Smock** with **G/K43**.

8. **Camouflage Uniform Cloth** in the second camouflage pattern. The white side is shown on the **Cuff Adjustment Strap**.

9. The camou-
flage side of the
**Winter Over-
Uniform.**

10. **Camou-
flage Uniform
Cloth** in the
first camou-
flage pattern.
**Uniform Lining
Cloth** of artifi-
cial silk.

11. A field-made **Camouflage M44 Field Service Tunic, Trousers** and **Helmet Cover** in the Waffen SS pattern.

12. **Waterproof Cloth** as used in the Shelter Quarter.

13. **M44 Field Service Tunic** with **Woven National Insignia** and **M43 Field Cap.**

14. Artificial cotton **Uniform Lining Cloth.**

15. **Twill Cloth of 1943-45** as used as uniform lining reinforcement.

16. A comparison of **Pre-1942 Woolen Uniform Cloth** and **1944-45 Uniform Cloth**.

17. A Panzer-faust 60M and MP/StG44.

18. Woolen Uniform Cloth of 1942-43. Artificial silk Uniform Lining Cloth.

19. An enameled
steel **Canteen**.

20. Outside view
of individual
equipment.

21. Web Equipment Harness and Fabric 1943-45.

22. Inside view of individual equipment.

23./24. Web individual equipment and **Combat Assault Pack, Wooden Tent Poles, Metal Tent Pins** and orange **Bakelite Canteen Cup.**

The Combat Assault Pack was a web frame used by the combat foot soldier to carry essential personal equipment into action. The Assault Pack was designed specifically for use with the Dismounted style of Cartridge Belt Suspenders and eased the carrying of the Shelter Quarter with tent pole and pins, the Mess Kit, the Greatcoat and/or Blanket. These items were strapped to the Combat Assault Pack with leather or web straps. While specific guidelines for proper placement of this gear were provided, the combat loads were tailored to the needs of the individual foot soldier.

Attached to the Combat Assault Pack, but generally unseen under the Shelter Quarter, was a small bag which could contain

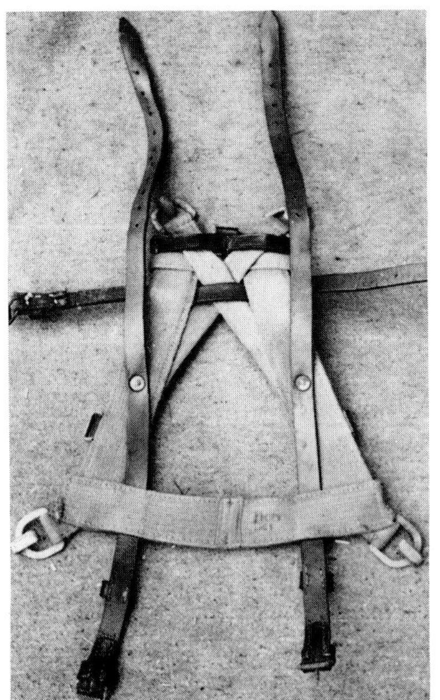

The front details of the **Combat Assault Pack**. For details of the rear portion see Vol. II.

"iron rations" (a small pre-packaged ration consisting of pre-served biscuits, meat, vegetables, coffee, and salt), individual weapon cleaning kit, sweater, or any small items that would not fit into the Bread Bag or pockets.

When carried, the Combat Assault Pack was attached to the D-rings on the Cartridge-Belt Suspender shoulder-straps, and secured with the lower pack-attachment straps.

The interior details of the **Combat Assault Pack Bag.** For other details see Vol. I and Vol. II.

Lernen durch Erfahrung
The Combat Assault Pack

The Combat Assault Pack is ink-stamped on one of the major web frame members or stamped into the leather utility straps. The bag is stamped in ink with the manufacturer's mark or code and date of production.

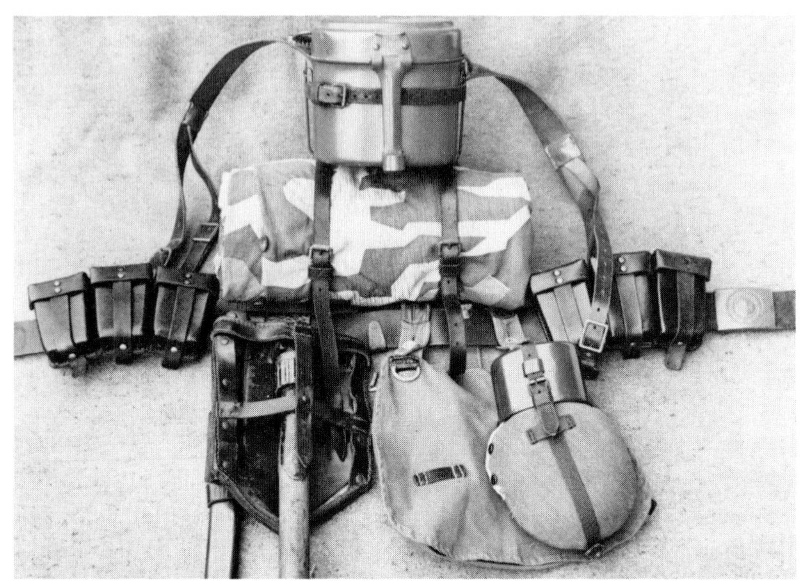

Front details of a soldier's completely assembled equipment. Of special interest is the enameled steel **Mess Kit**, dated 1944, and the late issue **Canteen**.

Rear details of a soldier's completely assembled equipment. Of interest is the bayonet scabbard retaining loop on the rear of the **Entrenching Tool Carrier**.

The Rucksack was designed to be used in the tropical theaters of war in place of the Model 1939 Rucksack. By 1944 and 1945 the Rucksack was used by foot soldiers on all fronts.

The Rucksack was constructed with minor war-time production modifications, but was basically a strong fabric bag equipped for attachment to the D-rings on Cartridge Belt Suspenders. The Rucksack generally had two flapped outer pockets closed by web or leather straps. The Rucksack neck was closed by a drawstring, and there was a large flap that was secured over the neck with a web or leather strap. Web or leather loops were sewn on the sides of the Rucksack to attach other items such as blanket rolls or skis.

Attachment hooks were sewn to upper and lower corners of the Rucksack to make it easier to carry on the Cartridge Belt Suspenders. D-rings were sewn on to the cover flap to allow the

The **Rucksack** here is shown being prepared for a march. The loaded **Rucksack** is attached to the **Cartridge Belt Suspenders**.

Combat Assault Pack to be carried on it in the same manner as the M39 Rucksack. A large metal attaching ring at the top of the Rucksack made it easy to hang up or transport when it was not being worn.

The interior of the Rucksack had a button-down pocket sewn onto the back to hold the Mess Kit. Two other internal button-down pockets were sewn onto the front panel of the Rucksack to securely store other small items.

The Rucksack with its large capacity and the security of its "sack" design made it a very practical piece of equipment which was widely used by the German foot soldier through the end of the war.

The **Rucksack** is prepared for march. The loaded **Combat Assault Pack** is hooked onto the **Rucksack** by means of provided D-rings. Of special interest is the large transport D-ring and the laminated wood **Canteen** with web straps.

Lernen durch Erfahrung
The Rucksack

The Rucksack is marked with an ink stamp with the manufacturer's code and production date or RB Nr. There is no general location in which the stamp is always placed.

In addition to the Rucksack that the German foot soldier was issued, he also received a Clothing Bag. The Clothing Bag of 1944-45 was made of strong, olive-colored fabric, much like the Bread Bag, with leather fastening straps and carrying handle.

The Clothing Bag was normally kept with the company supply trains. Items kept in the bag were those not required for daily front line life, such as seasonal or extra uniform pieces.

This **Clothing Bag** is ready for leave. Perhaps it is filled with carefully saved rations or perhaps gifts from a strange land.

The Model 1938 Gasmask and Canister

The Model 1938 Gasmask, or GM38, was made of synthetic rubber and was fitted with either the FE41 or FE42 filter element. The long web strap on the mask was used to suspend the mask around the neck in the ready position.

The fluted metal Canister with a spring-loaded lid catch contained the mask when it was not in use. A small box on the inside of the lid of the Canister contained replacement lens covers. A cleaning cloth was carried in the bottom of the Canister. Soldiers often carried a spare field dressing inside the Canister, on top of the mask. The number painted on the mask and on the Canister corresponded to the mask number placed in the foot soldier's Soldbuch (Identification, Record and Service Book).

The Canister found many uses aside from the one it was designed for. The stout construction enabled the carrying of

The **Model 1938 Gasmask** and **Canister** are shown here. Of interest is the cleaning cloth located in the bottom of the **Carrying Canister.**

precious bottles, and other consumables or items of high value. Loss or misuse of either the mask or the Canister was punishable, so great care had to be exercised when unauthorized practices were occurring.

The Gas-Cape or Gas-Sheet (a chemically-treated cloth or paper sheet used to cover the body for immediate protection in event of a gas attack) was contained in a rectangular cloth bag which was fixed to the Canister strap. The Gas-Cape Bag was positioned and carried on the front of the body. This carry position was later modified to one of securing the bag on the rear of the Canister strap, next to the Canister.

The Gas-Cape Bag was also strapped to the Canister with a leather strap. This was not an authorized method of carry and was forbidden. The Gas-Cape Bag was an extremely awkward item to carry in any of its regulation positions. The correction of this problem and the foot soldier's concern for chemical warfare by 1944 and 1945 was reflected in this style of portage and disregard of regulation.

Special eyeglasses (for those with impaired vision) were developed for use inside the mask. These glasses were identified as such by the designation printed on their grey metal carrying case.

The details of the spring-loaded closing catch. Of interest is the regularly practiced, but completely unauthorized, method of attaching the **Gas-Cape Bag** to the **Canister** by means of a leather strap. For other details see Vol. I and Vol. II.

The interior details of
the **Model 1938**
Gasmask.

The Model 1938 Gasmask and Canister

The Model 1938 Gasmask and Canister has a myriad of stamps and dates. The mask itself has the following stamps: on the rubber face piece there is an ink stamp showing date of manufacture; on the metal nosepiece there is usually a date in a circle and manufacturer's mark or code; the eyepieces are marked with the date of manufacture.

The Canister is stamped on the cover of the compartment which holds the spare lens inserts with a date of manufacture. There is also a "waffenamt" ink stamp in the same location plus a similar ink stamp on the bottom of the Canister, this stamp is very quickly worn off with use. Each of the Canister straps is ink-stamped with the manufacturer's code and date of production; this same information being part of the molded rubber ends on later production straps. If the Canister is of early production and still has its three leather strap protectors, each will have a manufacturer's mark or code and date stamped on it.

The mask filter is ink-stamped with a "waffenamt" manufacturer's code, and date of production. The filter also has the filter element-type stamped into the metal, i.e. FE41 or FE42.

The Ardennes Offensive

After fighting against the Americans near Aachen for several months, our regiment was pulled out of the line in early December and sent to Blankenheim to rest and refit. In the forest to the north of the town, we worked on our equipment and prepared for our next action against the Americans. As it was nearing Christmas, we all began to feel the pangs of homesickness; and hopes were high that perhaps, just perhaps, we might be overlooked for a little while and could spend Christmas in peace.

Our first hint that something new was in the air was our divisional night movement to the town of Scheid. Our worst fears of going back into combat were confirmed by a night march into an assembly area during the nights of 13 and 14 December. We had received large supplies of ammunition and rations, so we knew that action was close at hand.

During the day of December 15 we stayed in hidden positions in our assembly area. We were forbidden to make any fires or to make any noise. The sergeants and officers kept checking on us to ensure that we maintained a low profile. During this time most of the men in my squad wrote letters home. Christmas homesickness was turning into a major illness! Talk of going to the medics with symptoms went round and round in our squad.

Rations for our evening meal of December 15th were hot. We were astounded as we had expected only cold food. Around midnight our sergeant came to us. With him was our company commander. As we listened, our commander told us of the job we were about to undertake. We were about to end the war in the west!

I had been with the 27th Fusilier Regiment of the 12th Infantry Division since the late summer of 1944. The division was undergoing rebuilding after hard fighting in the east. The division was called the "Wild Buffalos" because of their hard charging style of the early war years. In September we moved on trains from East Prussia, where we had been rebuilding, and moved across Germany to the front near Aachen. We unloaded our vehicles and equipment in the town of Duren. We fought in the battle of the Huertgen Forest until early December. After

Waiting for the offensive.

this time our division was renamed the 12th Volksgrenadier Division because of the way we fought in the Huertgen Forest.

Our experience with the Americans in the Huertgen Forest had taught us that as long as the weather kept the enemy "Jabos" off our backs and the terrain kept the enemy tanks out of action we could defeat the Americans. The Huertgen Forest had given us a feeling that we could beat the Americans and that, given the right circumstances, we could throw them back into France and the sea!

The night of December 15th we were given the right circumstances. Our commander told us that a great army was massed to strike at the American lines. We would smash through the "fat sparrows" and seize Antwerp. This would cut the American and British Armies in half and take away one of their decisive supply ports. He told us that on our side were the elements of weather and total surprise. The ground was hard, the clouds and fog low to the ground. Our commander told us that the battle would open with a massive artillery bombardment that would destroy the American positions and render them incapable of fighting. Our new "Vengeance" weapons would bombard their rear areas and our air force, armed with new, high-speed aircraft would keep the sky clear of enemy "Jabos" and provide close support for our advance.

The "old hares" were very excited and talked of the way it used to be in 1940, 41, and 42. Now it would again be the same for the German army...VICTORY!

Our sergeant told us that we would have to attack without mercy and keep going no matter what the cost. I recall that I thought about the bombing of my home and town by the American Air Force. My Mother and sisters were safe, but without a place to live during the winter. Others were not so fortunate and had lost loved ones. Now we could smash the invaders and put a stop to the war. Each of us knew what he must do and we steeled ourselves and each other for what would lie ahead.

After midnight our company made ready to move into assault position. We were told to make sure our equipment was secure so that we would not make noise when we marched. We checked our equipment and our weapons over and over again. Moving slowly and quietly, we took up our positions and waited for the assault.

At 0530 on the 16th of December the attack began with the thundering of what seemed like a thousand cannons. The sky to our rear was lit by the muzzle blasts. The dark of night was changed instantly by the beams of searchlights, shone onto clouds over the enemy positions in Losheim. Here in Losheim was where we first struck at the enemy.

After taking Losheim, we pushed northwest along the railroad tracks towards Bullingen. As we pressed on towards our objective, we ran into some very heavy resistance from some American infantry in and around the railway station of Buchholtz. This resistance was stout and required some time to put down. By evening we had overcome the Americans at Buchholtz, and we were at the western edge of the Schlieden Forest overlooking the town of Hunningen.

We paused here in the forest, as night had fallen, preparing for the next assault on the Americans in Hunningen. Our attack was preceded by a bombardment by our artillery. As we began to move across the fields, we began to receive incoming artillery fire which seemed to move with us as we worked towards the enemy lines. Our sergeant kept at us to stay ahead of the artillery fire. Because our sergeant pushed us hard and made use of every bit of cover he could find for us as we rushed across the open areas, we avoided casualties in our squad. We reached the first buildings at the southwest edge of town and raced through American fire across the bridge and into the town.

The Americans in Hunningen were putting up even stiffer resistance than those at Buchholtz. The American artillery was shooting at and hitting our troops without difficulty. There was no sign of any high speed aircraft to attack the American cannons. We fought through the town until the afternoon when the American resistance began to fade. Confident of our victory here our commander ordered us to push quickly to the north end of town. Here, as the light of day began to fade, the battle to end the war ended for me.

The Americans were fighting and withdrawing towards the north to another town on the next ridge. As we pressed their rear guard, the American artillery again began to bombard the edge of Hunningen. The first shells crashed into the buildings near our squad, and I was severely wounded in the body and on the arms by shell fragments and debris. I was struck in the head by a large piece of brick, but my helmet saved my skull.

My comrades stuck by me until our medics came. I gave my money and rations to my sergeant, because I knew these would be stolen the first moment I was unconcious. I had an American pistol that I had picked up the day before in Losheim. This I gave to my best friend. My comrades kept up the jokes about hospitals and nurses until the medic had covered my wounds. I said goodby just as our platoon sergeant came to check on the squad's progress. He told the medic to see I was well cared for. Since my legs had not been wounded, the medic told me to walk to the battalion first aid station. The medic at the battalion aid station sent me to the regimental aid station. Here the medic checked my bandages and sent me on to the rear on foot with other walking wounded. We were directed to the main dressing station where the doctor checked my wounds and gave me a shot to prevent infection and a shot to ease my pain. That evening I was evacuated to the railroad station and put on a train to go to a general hospital for treatment and recovery.

I recovered from my wounds and received the Wound Badge in Black. I was only hospitalized for seven weeks, so I was able to return to my regiment and comrades. By now the great "von Rundstedt Offensive" had failed and had taken many of the lives of my comrades. Now, we who survived fought to survive the final months and days of the combat as the enemy pushed deeper and deeper into Germany.

Through the gate and into the Main Dressing Station.

The Weapons

This tank hunting team is preparing to engage a target.

Knives

Few pieces of equipment meant as much to a German foot soldier as his knife. Large or small, fixed or folding blade, the knife was a solid and dependable companion.

In addition to the bayonet, the foot soldier could be issued two basic types of knives: the folding style utility knife and the fixed blade combat knife.

The basic issue, utility, pocket knife came in several forms. The issue knives were produced by various factories in the city of Solingen, or in factories of occupied or Allied nations. This diverse production coupled with wartime needs and changes resulted in varied knives. The folding utility knife was viewed as a tool more than a weapon. To this end, a knife that contained valuable implements essential to daily life was highly prized. Folding knives were found with single, main blades, some of which were locking by design. Knives were found with long and short blade combinations. Some knives had blades and a very valuable corkscrew. Folding knives were produced with these plus other implements such as a can opener and an awl. The

Issue and privately purchased folding **Knives.**

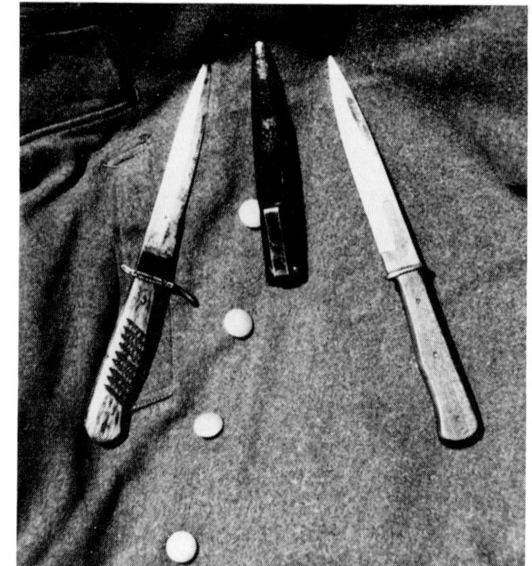

Two styles of fixed
blade combat knife and
one metal sheath with
a clip attachment.

folding utility knife had a handgrip of either wood, bakelite plastic or bare metal depending on design, period of the war and manufacture.

The basic fixed blade combat knife was a weapon of well-thought-out and lethal design. Patterned after the hunting daggers used by German men throughout the centuries, the combat knife became a production and issue item during the 1914-1918 conflict. The need for a combat knife in the 1939-1945 conflict brought the old designs off the factory shelves, and with some modifications, by 1944 and 1945 the combat knife was an essential part of the foot soldier's equipment. The combat knife style was not attractive, only functional. The blade was sharpened fully on one side and partially on the other. There was very little hilt and the hand grips were of plain wood riveted to the blade tang. The sheaths were usually produced of stamped metal with clip attachments provided to mount them in the boot top, in the service uniform or on the equipment.

Both styles of issue knives had private purchase counterparts and these were often carried because of their proven worth, for good luck or for sentimental reasons. Knives of the enemy, captured in battle, were also carried and used. These trusted companions stayed with their owners when all else was lost or taken.

The 7.92mm Model Kar.98k Rifle

Caliber: 7.92mm
Length: 43.6 inches
Weight: 8 lbs., 9 oz.
Magazine and capacity: Five-round internal box magazine loaded with loose rounds or five-round stripper clips.
Operation: Mauser patent bolt action.

The Kar.98k was the last in a long line of German military rifles based on the Gewehr-98 of 1898. The Kar.98k was adopted for use by the German Army in 1935 and continued in service until the end of the conflict in 1945.

The war years brought small changes in manufacture technique and quality of this weapon. The most significant change was the elimination of the bayonet lug and cleaning rod along with increased use of stamped fixtures and less finishing. Although plans were made to replace the Kar.98k with other weapons which would increase the firepower of the foot soldier and reduce construction costs, it was never replaced as the primary weapon of the German foot soldier.

The 7.92mm Model Kar.98k Rifle with ZF.41 Telescopic Rifle Sight

The 7.92mm Model Kar. 98k used with the ZF. 41 Telescopic Sight was nearly identical to the standard Kar.98k rifle used by any foot soldier, except that this weapon had a short dovetail rail machined out of the left side of the rear sight band. This rail was used to mount the telescopic sight to the rifle by means of a spring-loaded clamp.

The combination of the ZF. 41 with the Kar.98k was not considered a sniper rifle; instead it was considered as an improved weapons' system for the average foot soldier.

When the ZF.41 Telescopic Sight was not being used, it was carried in a small olive- or tan-colored can that was affixed to the Cartridge Belt by means of a web or leather belt loop.

In 1944 and 1945, the ZF. 41 with the Kar.98k was still the only improved weapons system available to the average foot soldier. The G43 with the ZF. 41 Telescopic Sight was considered a proper sniping system and was kept in the hands of these sharpshooters.

The **7.92mm Model Kar.98k Rifle with ZF.41 Telescopic Sight**. For more details on **Rifle** and **Scope** see Vol. I and Vol. II.

The 7.92mm Model 41
Semi-Automatic Rifle (G41)

Caliber: 7.92mm
Length: 44.5 inches
Weight: 11.0lb
Magazine and capacity: 10-round internal box-magazine charged with two five-round stripper clips.
Operation: gas operated, self-loading, semi-automatic
The G41 was a result of the German Army's desire to produce a self-loading rifle to replace the Kar.98k. The concept, first explored in 1937, came to fruition in designs by both the Walther and Mauser firms. The Mauser design failed to meet testing standards and was scrapped. The Walther design was produced, in limited numbers, and was not widely used or well-liked.

The 7.92mm Model 43
Semi-Automatic Rifle (G/K43)

Caliber: 7.92mm
Length: 44.0 inches
Weight: 9lb 9oz
Barrel length: 22 inches
Magazine and capacity: 10-round detachable box charged with either loose rounds or with two five-round stripper clips.

The Gewehr 43 was a further step forward in the design of a successful self-loading rifle. Taking the experiences of war from the Gewehr 41 (W) and (M), Walther developed the concept further and produced a specialist weapon which was generally used for sniping on all fronts.

The bolt locking system was similar to that invented by Friberg Kjellman, whereby the firing pin pushed a pair of hinged flaps on the bolt into recesses in the body, just before it struck the primer in the cartridge case. This method of loading was identical to that on the Gew 41(W), however, the gas system was radically altered. Various Tokarev designs were studied, and eventually the gas cylinder was placed above the barrel. During firing, some of the gases were bled off through a gas port, onto a cup shaped piston thus unlocking the breech.

Officially accepted into service on the 30th of April 1943, the G/K43 served in relatively small numbers right up to the end of the war, even though it was superceded in May 1944 by the MP43/StG44.

With the development of the MP43/StG44, the planned rearmament of the German foot soldier with a self-loading weapon was again changed. Neither of these options was ever fully realized and the G43 continued in limited use with the foot soldier until 1945.

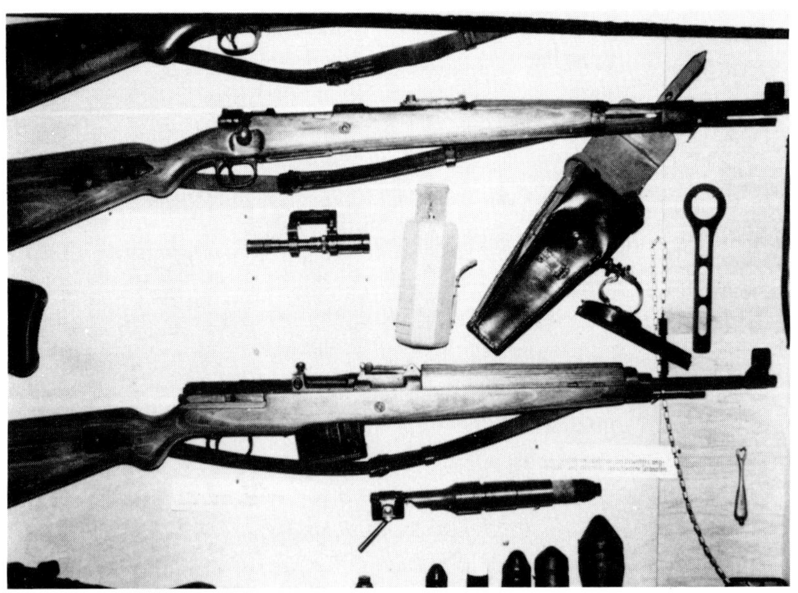

The **7.92mm Model 43 Semi-automatic Rifle** or **G/K43.**

Details of the sight, magazine and upper receiver of the **G/K43**.

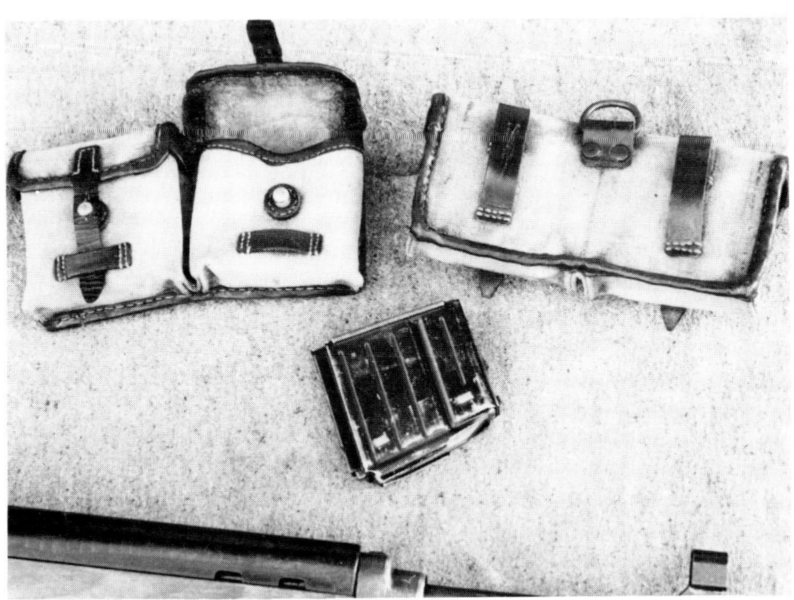

Details of the magazine pouches, the 10-round magazine and the barrel area of the **G/K43**.

The Machine Pistol MP43, 43/1, 44
or Assault Rifle 44

Details of both sides of the **MP44/StG44**.

Caliber: 7.92mm "Short" cartridge (Pistol Cartridge 43)
Length: 37.0 inches
Weight: 11.25 lbs.
Magazine and capacity: 30 round detachable curved box magazine, charged with stripper clips
Barrel Length: 16.5 inches
Cyclic rate of fire: 500 rounds per minute
Operation: gas operated, tripping bolt, selective fire

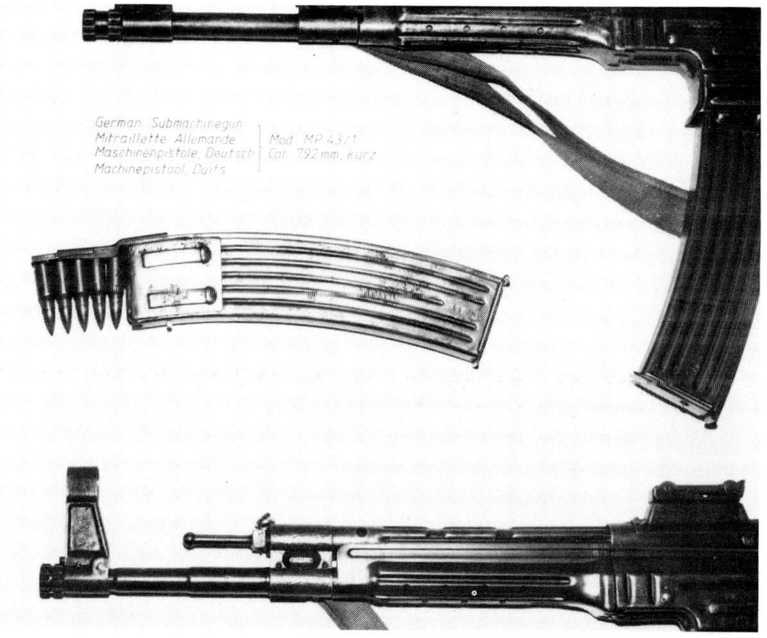

Details of the magazine of the **MP44/StG44** and of the upper and lower forward portions of the weapon.

During 1940 to 1941 Louis Schmeisser designed a self-loading rifle designated the MKb42(H) at the Haenel weapons and bicycles factory in Suhl. Eight thousand of these rifles were produced for trial at the Russian front during November 1942 to April 1943.

Further development and minor design changes, such as the removal of the bayonet lug and repositioning of the gas block, resulted in the appearance of the MP43 in July of that year.

Towards the end of August 1943, production was undertaken at a variety of factories in Germany, by now a common practice in the strife to increase manufacturing output in view of heavier bombing raids on towns and cities by the Allies.

Expanding on their experience in production techniques, they manufactured the MP43 almost exclusively from stamped and pressed steel. They simplified fastening methods by using rivets, pins and clip springs instead of screws, crimping instead of soldering, and die casting instead of forging. They used plastics and later beech and ash for the furniture.

The **7.92mm "Short" Cartridge** for the MP44/StG44. The ammunition came loaded in five-round stripper clips, packed in cardboard boxes as shown here. The magazines were loaded from the stripper clips by using a special loading tool.

Generally very successful, well-liked and guarded by those fortunate enough to have been issued it, the MP43 was further modified in late 1943 when a telescopic sight-mounting bracket was added, and the muzzle of the barrel threaded to accept a new screw-on type of grenade launcher. This, then, became the MP43/1. During April 1944, the designation was changed to MP44 as a result of alterations in dimensions to several internal components making them incompatible with the MP43/1.

During a demonstration of assault tactics on the vast ranges at Bergen Hohne, Hitler was first introduced to the MP43, MP43/1, MP44, and in his enthusiasm of observing assaulting infantry, suggested the term Sturmgeweher as a more appropriate term than MP. Hence the final redesignation to StG44.

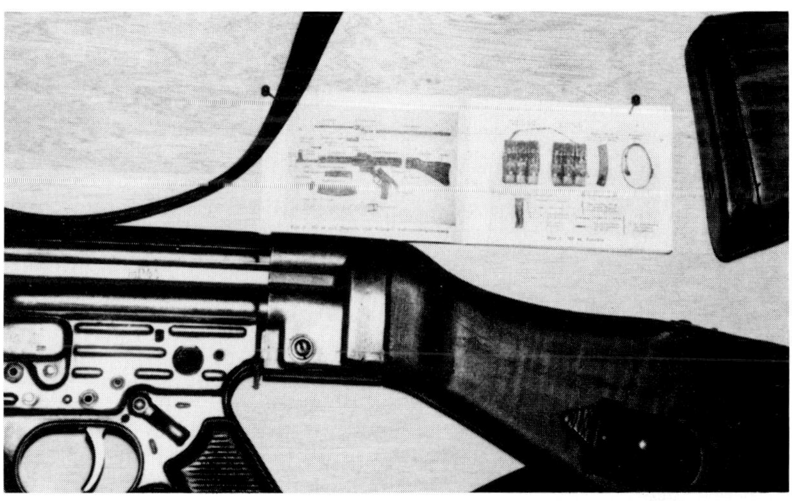

Each MP44/StG44 was issued with an instruction booklet as shown here. Also of interest is the lower receiver area and selective fire switch.

The Machine Pistol MP40 and 40/II

Caliber: 9mm Parabellum
Length with stock folded: 24.75 inches
Length with stock unfolded: 32.75 inches
Weight: 9 lbs.
Barrel length: 9.75 inches
Magazine capacity: 32 rounds in a box magazine
Operation: Blowback, automatic fire only.

Commonly, though incorrectly, known as the "Schmeisser," the MP40 was a submachine gun which found its origin in the MP38. This gun was designed and built by the Erma factory in Erfurt, Germany, at a time when Hugo Schmeisser was employed elsewhere.

This **MP40** is being fired from the shoulder, as this soldier suppresses the enemy.

Following the methodical German practice of designating firearms with the year of entry into service, the MP40 was introduced to save the high manufacturing costs of the MP38, and to increase production. This was achieved by using low grade steel, omitting some components, simplifying the construction, and thereby reducing the number of machining operations required.

With an increase in tolerances, it was possible to subcontract all work to factories throughout the Third Reich, with final assembly carried out in relatively few factories, where most of the spot welding and brazing of the stampings was done.

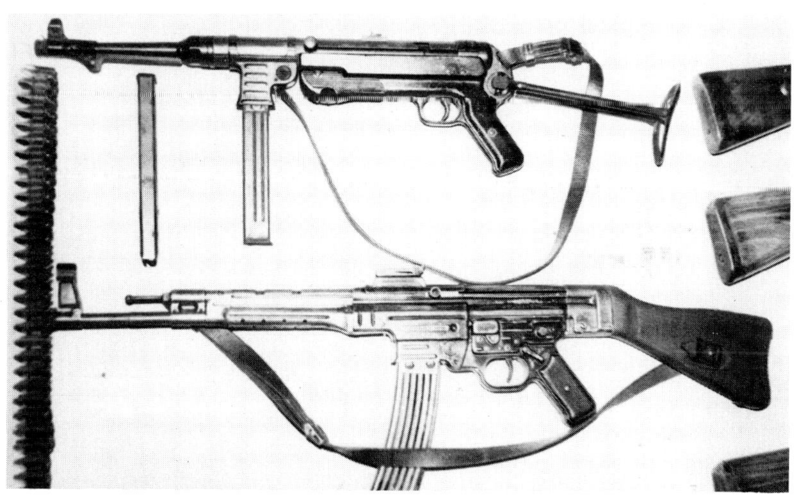

The **Machine Pistol MP40** and extra magazine.

The MP40 was the first of its kind to use early plastics technology in the manufacture of the fore end and pistol grips. The phenol resin and paper fibre filling was durable and resisted most knocks and bangs, but was almost impossible to repair successfully by the "Waffenmeister."

Overall, the MP40 was a very successful design which lent itself well to the tactical doctrine of the German Armored Infantry.

Though not the only derivative, the MP40/II is the most interesting in that it had two magazines fitted. During 1942 and 1943 the Russians were using a 71-round magazine. The Germans tried to compensate for this with a modified magazine housing and a shuttle into which two thirty-two round magazines were fitted. When the shuttle was knocked over to the right, the bolt could fire rounds from the left magazine. With the shuttle to the left the opposite was true. Magazine catches were fitted to the shuttle. This was not a successful design, since it became easy to knock the shuttle and the magazine out of the path of the bolt causing stoppages. Also, at twelve pounds the weapon was too heavy, which defeated the object of producing a light automatic weapon. Although the exact number is not known, very few MP40/IIs were made.

The Rifle Grenade-Launcher

The standard method for firing rifle grenades was use of the Rifle Grenade-Launcher. Having a rifled discharger cup of 3 cm. caliber, the launcher was attached to the barrel of the Kar.98k, the G43/K43, or the MP43/StG44 (with use of a modified propelling cartridge) by means of a quick-clamping system. The grenade propellant charge was packed in a special bulletless rifle cartridge, which came with each grenade. The launcher body

The **Rifle Grenade-Launcher** and **Grenades**. From left to right: the **High Explosive Rifle Grenade**, the **Anti-Tank Rifl Grenade**, the **Illuminating Parachute Rifle Grenade**, the **Large Anti-Tank Grenade**, the **46mm Hollow-Charge Rifle Grenade**, and the **S.S. 61mm Hollow-Charge Rifle Grenade**. Also shown are the propellant charges and cardboard containers.

screwed together to form a tight fit around the grenade.

Aiming of the weapon was accomplished by means of a tangent sight attached to the rifle near the bolt action. Various styles of grenades were developed for use with the Rifle Grenade-Launcher to include high-explosive, anti-tank, smoke, illumination and leaflet. Enemy troop targets could be engaged at up to 275 meters and enemy armor could be engaged at up to 100 meters with the exception of the SS Gew Panzergranat 61 grenade, which doubled that range. The grenade and propelling bullet were packaged together in individual cardboard containers.

The entire Rifle Grenade-Launcher set was contained and carried in a leather pouch with a web strap.

The 7.92mm Machine Gun Model 1942 (MG42)

Caliber: 7.92mm
Length: 48.0 inches
Weight: 25 lbs. 8 oz.
Barrel length: 21.0 inches
Cyclic rate of fire: 1,200 rounds per minute
Feed system: linked belts, or fifty-round belt in drum magazine.
Operation: recoil, gas assisted

These **MG42**s show details of both sides of the machine gun. The bipods are shown in the extended and folded positions. A belt of ammunition is shown, loaded and ready for firing.

In 1941, the German army was critically short of small arms, particularly an efficient machine gun for the infantry, as industry and resources were directed primarily towards the construction of capital equipment like tanks and aircraft. Radical ideas brought out the concept of one machine gun to fulfill all roles. Combining the success of the MG34 and the manufacturing techniques perfected in making the MP40, the MG42 was born. The MG42 was first produced at the Mauser Works in Spandau, Berlin, hence its nickname "Spandau."

Although similar to the MG34 in many respects, the locking system was new. The bolt was locked in the body by means of rollers which engaged cammed faces. Upon firing, the bolt remained closed by virtue of the angles on the cammed recesses. Only when the pressure of the propellant gasses was reduced to

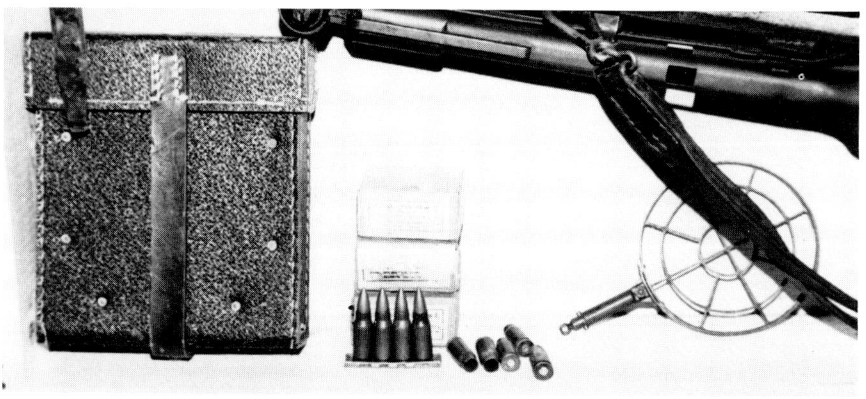

The **Accessory Pouch** for the MG42. This pouch contained items necessary for operation and maintenance of the gun. The anti-aircraft sight (shown) was carried here. The ammunition is for a MP43/StG44.

A spare **Barrel Case** and an **Ammunition Box** for the MG42.

a safe level, did they act on the concave face in the barrel bearing, imparting a sharp thrust on the face of the barrel which in turn unlocked the breech.

Considering the very high rate of fire, the barrel soon got hot. By means of a simple latch, the barrel could be disengaged from the weapon and withdrawn from the right, through the long cut away portion of the receiver, and a fresh barrel installed.

During numerous heavy infantry engagements on the Eastern Front, it was not unusual for a tripod-mounted gun to fire continuous belts of ammunition until the barrels became shot out, somewhere in the region of 10,000 rounds.

This weapon was so successful, that after the war, the Allies sold many thousands to African and South American countries. The Allies even copied many of the design features of the MG42 to produce weapons like the FN MAG, the M60. Even the West German Army uses it today in only a slightly modified form known as the MG3A1.

The Reinforced Squad Strongpoint

The smallest element in the defense of any position was the squad. The squad strongpoint was the first link in the chain of defense and was incorporated into the platoon, company and battalion defense plan.

The reinforced squad strongpoint was designed and constructed for all-around defense. The point was surrounded by barbed-wire obstacles, various antipersonnel and antitank mines. The Reinforced Squad Strongpoint contained one or more company and/or battalion heavy weapons such as additional machine guns, mortars or antitank weapons. In addition, the strongpoint and the area is occupied was covered by a pre-plotted regimental, and perhaps divisional, artillery fire plan.

When establishing a Reinforced Squad Strongpoint, it was essential to make the most of the land to provide necessary cover and concealment. This move limited the enemy's observation and provided the position with the added strength of surprise. Positions placed without the use of the land, where they could be seen by the enemy, were usually destroyed by mass enemy fire! Strongpoints positioned in a wooded area required more time to complete, but provided excellent concealment and cover.

Strongpoints were built according to the rule: "First be ready to affect the enemy with your position before being worried about how enemy action may affect your position." This meant that first, combat trenches were built, barbed wire was put up and landmines were laid in. Later, the machine-gun and the anti-tank positions were built.

The fields of fire were cleared around the Strongpoint, but this was done so as not to sacrifice concealment! If possible one to three meters of underbrush were left between the Strongpoint and the enemy! The wire obstacles and earthworks of the Strongpoint were built along the natural lines of the ground, such as hedgerows or edges of fields. Trenches were dug in a zigzag at obtuse angles. Excavated earth from the trenches and dugouts was placed behind the positions to block out the foot soldiers' silhouette.

Dugouts were dug deep, with at least three layers of earth and logs on top to protect the soldiers from enemy artillery and mortar fire! Forward listening and observation posts were placed well to the front of the Strongpoint. These were linked by field telephones or radios.

The Stick Grenade Model 39

The M39 Stick Grenade was the standard hand grenade of the German Army throughout the War. The grenade consisted of a thin, metal, explosive-filled, cylindrical head that was screwed onto a hollow wooden handle. A friction pull-igniter activated the timed fuse when a cord (ending in a porcelain ball) was pulled. The grenade was kept in the "safe" condition by use of a screw-off end-cap on the wooden handle, which kept the porcelain ball and igniter pull cord safely inside the handle.

The M39 could be used as an offensive grenade, designed to injure or kill the enemy with concussion, not fragments, in order to allow the safe advance of German forces. If fragmentation was desired in defensive action, a smooth or segmented steel sleeve could be slipped over the grenade head. The fuse time was 4-5 seconds.

Stopping an enemy advance with grenades. Of interest is the cord in the hand of the soldier in front. When this cord is pulled, the grenade is armed.

The Stick Grenade Model 43

In 1943 a similar-looking stick grenade appeared, the Model 43. It had a solid wood handle, with a blue-capped pull igniter screwed into the top of the grenade head. Smooth or segmented fragmentation sleeves could be fitted.

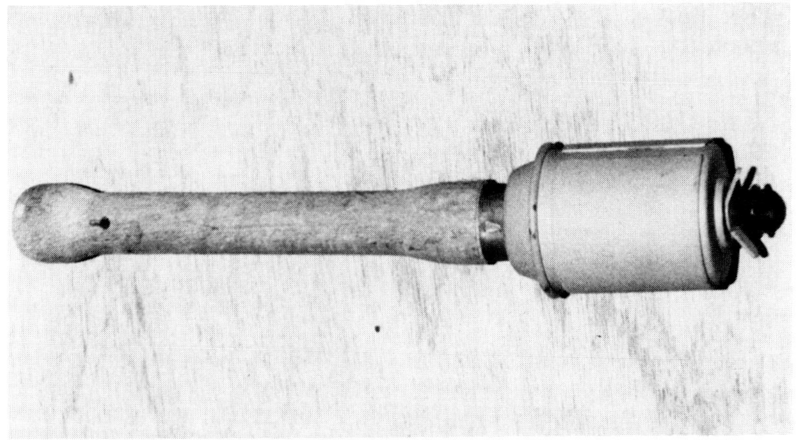

The **Stick Grenade Model 43**. For more details of grenades, see Vol. I and Vol. II.

The Egg Grenade Model 39

The M39 Egg Grenade was designed as an offensive weapon. The thin metal body was filled with a high proportion of high explosive. The grenade was armed by unscrewing the cap and then pulling the cap away from the grenade body. This activated the friction igniter in the grenade. An egg-shaped fragmentation sleeve was developed to adapt the grenade to defensive use. Fuse time was 4-5 seconds.

The lack of an individual weapon that would allow the foot soldier to attack and defeat Soviet armor brought about the development of the Panzerfaust. The Panzerfaust was a recoilless, single-shot, anti-tank weapon that launched a fin-stabilized shaped-charge bomb. The launcher section of the Panzerfaust was a milled steel tube that contained a propellant charge, and mounted the aiming and firing devices for the weapon. The launcher allowed the foot soldier to hold and aim the Panzerfaust. Once fired, the launcher was discarded. Panzerfaust de-

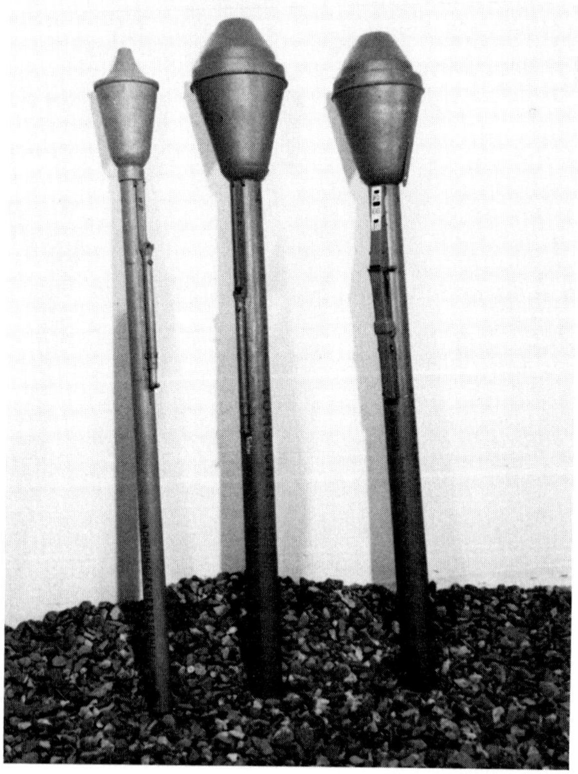

Three examples of **Panzerfausts**, from left to right: the **Panzerfaust Klein 30M**, the **Panzerfaust 30M**, and the **Panzerfaust 60M**.

velopment continued through October of 1943 when the first version was put into production.

The first version was known as the Panzerfaust 30M and could launch its bomb to a distance of 30 meters. The charge in the bomb could penetrate and destroy all known Soviet armor. At the same time another version, the Panzerfaust "Klein" 30M, which had a less powerful warhead, was also put into production. While the penetration properties of the bombs were sufficient, the range of engagement was not, and improvements were called for.

Improvements came in the form of the Panzerfaust 60M in early 1944 and Panzerfaust 100M in November 1944. These new

The details of the bomb and of the trigger. Of interest are the numerous proofing stamps.

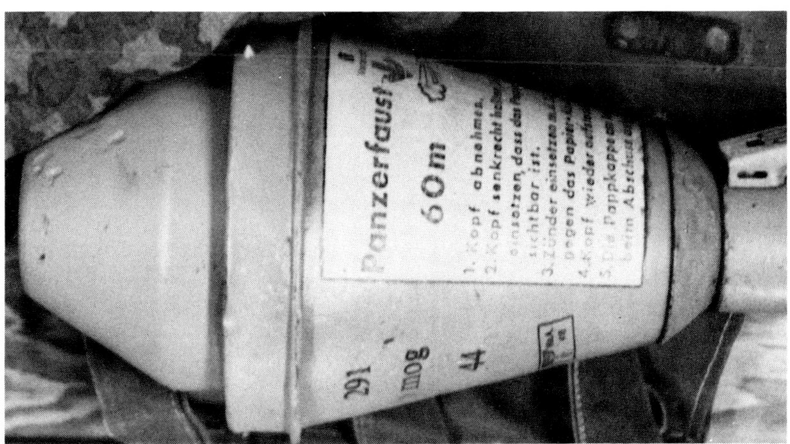

An "alte Hase" gives a lesson on the **Panzerfaust 60M**. He is pointing out the three range indicators on the raised sighting arm.

versions of the Panzerfaust allowed the foot soldier to attack enemy armor from a greater distance. With the advent of the 60M, production of the 30M series ended.

Further improvements in design produced the Panzerfaust 150M which made use of a re-loadable launcher and a bomb that had the propellant attached to its base. This weapon was produced in 1945, but transportation and supply difficulties restricted its use by foot soldiers.

The use of the Panzerfaust allowed more of the anti-armor role to be shifted from the anti-tank artillery and to be placed on the foot soldier. This was noticeable in the organizational make up of the new "Infantry Division 1944," the "Volks Grenadier" Divisions, and the "Infantry Division 1945."

Attacking Tanks

By 1944 and 1945 weapons enabling the engagement and defeat of enemy armored vehicles had come onto the scene. Now armed with Panzerfausts and Panzerschrecks, which could defeat any enemy tank, the foot soldier became an even more important part of a units anti-armor defense. The organizational tables of the new style infantry divisions of 1944 reflected this trend.

No matter how devastating the weapons provided the foot soldier were, the basic fact that a man had to face and defeat a machine remained unchanged. Close combat with tanks continued to be risky business until the war's finish.

The Panzerfaust in any of its version is an excellent anti-tank weapon. The Panzerfaust requires a bit of experience in order to get used to its battlefield performance. To engage an enemy tank with the Panzerfaust, you must be keen in your judgments of distance and of speed. In order to secure the best possible edge during an engagement, you must place yourself in favorable positions for battle.

The worst prospect for engaging a tank with a Panzerfaust is found wherever the tank's speed or range of engagement is greater than that of the tank hunter. Anything that proves an obstacle to the tank's movement or firepower is of benefit to the hunter.

Engaging tanks inside a town or city is the best of all possible situations. Here the tank is required to move at a slower rate of speed; the tank's weapon is only as good as the gunner's vision and there are many hiding places for the hunter.

Setting the trap for the enemy tank depends on the time available to the tank hunting team. With ample time the section can place anti-tank mines and barriers. With time the section can choose firing positions that are hidden and protected.

Hidden, protected positions help ensure a good killing shot by keeping the pressure off the hunter and allowing him to concentrate on the sighting and firing of his weapon. The best positions are on upper floors of buildings from windows that allow the hunter to observe his target from inside the room and to fire without exposing himself. The best time to fire is when the enemy has passed the hunter's position. This allows the bomb to strike the vehicle on its rear upper body sections, which are not thickly armored.

Simultaneous engagement by more than one hunter also helps to insure a favorable outcome for the tank-hunting team. The number of bombs in the cone of fire increases the probability of a hit on and destruction of the enemy tank.

The greatest threat to the tank-hunting team is that of enemy infantry. The combined use of foot soldiers and tanks makes the attack by the tank-hunting team more difficult. The observation of the infantry is keener and their reactions faster, enabling them to spot any error made by the hunters. In this situation the use of upper floors and planned escape routes through buildings serves the tank-hunters well.

This corporal is the loader for this Panzerschreck Tank Hunting Team. He is ready to load a 8.8cm rocket.

The 8.8cm Anti-Tank Rocket Launcher

Capture of the American "Bazooka" anti-tank weapon in the North African desert gave the German Army a much needed developmental boost in its search for a way to arm the foot soldier against Soviet armor. Working from the original American design, the Germans made their own improvements to create a very effective anti-tank weapon for the German foot soldier.

The three versions of the **8.8cm Anti-Tank Rocket Launcher,** from left to right: the **Model 54/1,** the **Model 54** and the **Model 43.**

The Tank Hunting Team prepares for a kill. Of interest is the blast shield on the launcher.

Fire! The **8.8cm Rocket** is on its way to the target! The smoke indicates a reason why this weapon was called the "Stovepipe." Now the team must withdraw as their position is compromised.

The German production 8.8cm Anti-Tank Rocket Launcher was known to the foot soldier as the Ofenrohr (Stovepipe) or Panzerschreck (Tank Terror). The Panzerschreck was initially issued in late 1943 in the first, or Model 1943, version. The Panzerschreck could fire a 8.8 cm rocket-propelled, hollow-charged projectile to a distance of 150 meters. The projectile could penetrate up to 100mm of armor with reasonable accuracy. The major drawback to the weapon was its emission of flame and smoke which required the use of special protective clothing for the operator and left a very visible launch signature.

In 1944 a shield was added to the Panzerschreck to eliminate the need for protective clothing for the operator. This improved version was designated Model 54. Further improvements in the design of the launcher and the missile in 1944 produced the final version of the Panzerschreck, the Model 54/1. The Model 54/1 used an improved projectile that increased the range of the weapon system to 180 meters.

The Panzerschreck remained in service until the end of the war. Towards the end, however, elements necessary for the creation of rocket propellent for the projectile became harder to get and emphasis was shifted to the Panzerfaust. Even so, use of the well-liked Panzerschreck by German foot soldiers continued until the close of hostilities in 1945.

Vocabulary of the Veteran Foot Soldier

The front-line foot soldier has a language of his own. The foot soldier develops this language to express his thoughts and desires to his comrades in a way unique to them. This language reflects a way of life in a sub-culture developed for, and by, men who have reduced life and its living to the most primitive elements.

The German foot soldier of 1944 and 1945 had his own language. Some examples are given here:

Fussfantrist: "foot soldier"

turmen: "to leg it" or run away from action.

mordererisher Kampf: "murderous battle" or severe fighting.

Grossschlacht: "Armageddon" or the final battle of the war.

Heimat-schuss: the wound that gets you sent home for good. By 1944 and 1945 near-permanent incapacitation was required

Abendsegen: "evening blessing" or the routine artillery or air attack by the enemy forces carried out in the evening. This was also called the "evening hate."

Morgensegen: "morning blessing", or the routine artillery or air attack by enemy forces carried out in the morning. This was also known as the "morning hate."

Alarm!: a command to fall in or to take ones battle position.

Alter: "old man" or the senior member of a group.

Alte Kampfer: "old fighter" or "old timer".

Alte Knochen: "old sweat", "tough veteran", or "old bones"

angewarmte Leiche: "a warmed-up corpse" or someone who is nearly out of action due to exhaustion or injury.

ausradieren: "wipe out" or to totally destroy a position.

Bach: "drink", usually a strong beer.

baden gehen: "to go swimming" or to go west and get out of the east front fighting. This term was first used in the early western campaigns with reference to going swimming in the English Channel.

Besetzt Zeichen: "engaged zone," the beaten zone of fire or an area of great danger.

Bonze: "a stuffed shirt" or a senior officer or official.

dran sein: "ones number is up" or in a position where there is no chance of survival.

Freiheits-Sender: "Freedom sender," a release from combat duty or "the Angel of Death."

Fuss latscher: "mud crusher" or foot slogger.

Hohes Tier: "highest animal" or top dog.

Heim im der Reich: "Home in Germany" or to go home.

Hunde-angst: "dogs fear" or to be so frightened that no rational action or reasoning is possible. This type of behavior is directly observable in dogs that are very frightened.

The *Soldat* Combat Uniform Collector's Planner

The successful completion of any military mission requires careful planning and execution. The maintenance of historical facts requires careful record keeping. The same holds true for the collection of combat uniforms.

Without careful record-keeping procedures, the collector can easily lose track of important acquisitions in his or her collection. As the years pass, a collection changes and grows. Many times I have looked back and wondered what exactly became of an item from my collection. Had I sold or traded it? As the years go by it is very interesting and financially wise to note the changes in value of collectible items. As collections grow, a comprehensive inventory is necessary for accountability in case of any unforeseen disaster!

Making and keeping a record of your collection is not difficult if done with a plan from the beginning. In the spirit of *Der alte Hase*, I am providing the following pages for the exclusive use of *Soldat* readers to help you begin and keep these records. Let me explain the individual pages and their uses to you.

The *Soldat* Collection Information Log

This log, when filled out, will provide you with all the essential physical and historical information you need about any item in your collection. The log also provides a reminder of items presently not in your collection. As items are bought and sold, traded and re-traded, the log pages will give you a historical record of your collection.

Aside from the information pertaining to the item itself, the log reminds you of the amount paid or traded, and where the item came from and when. Also noted is the item you may have traded to secure the new collectible. The log provides a means of "tracking" items that have left your collection, if other collectors use the same log. This information would allow you to find any item that was formerly in your collection.

The log also aids in the identification of reproductions and their sources. With record maintenance and comparison with other collectors' logs, persons who unwittingly or knowingly sell or trade reproductions can be spotted. This allows you to educate not only yourself about reproductions, but others as well. Persons who continually abuse other collectors by selling or trading reproductions as originals can be confronted with documented information of their activity.

The *Soldat* Collector's Roster

This page allows you to record all the practical information on any collector you have dealings with or with whom you no longer desire to have dealings. Specific notes pertaining to their collecting activities can be jotted down and kept as a lasting reminder of individuals you have or had had collecting activities with. Here again the maintenance of records will allow you to recall your contacts after many years and many transactions.

The *Soldat* Business Roster

Keeping a list of honest and fair businesses is essential. Any collector may find that the use of a dealer of militaria is required to fill a "hole" in their collection. The recording of both the upright, or more shady, of dealers will prevent costly future mistakes. Every collector finds him or herself in contact with other businesses, aside from dealers of militaria, in everyday collecting activities. Careful record-keeping and comparison will help you to ensure that you are doing the best you can for your hobby and other collectors.

The *Soldat* Veteran's Roster

The best source of any item for your collection is the veteran who either used it or brought it back as a war trophy. An honest veteran as a source of such items is the best contact you can have. In order to keep track of these veterans and what they maintain in their possession, I have provided two roster pages.

I enjoy the historical presence that a veteran can give to a piece of militaria, and I take notes about each encounter. I find these records allow me to remember the history of each item, whether it becomes part of my collection or not. For those who wish to account for all their financial dealings, I have provided a space for gift and correspondence costs. Unless you place historical value of an item higher than its market value, keeping tabs on your expenses is important.

The *Soldat* Collector's Bibliography Log

Quality reference books are a must for the collector. Knowing what you have in your collecting library is essential. With this page you know what books you have, where and how you came by them and where they went.

As the direction of your collection changes, books may be sold or traded. By knowing the publisher, a replacement can be ordered if the need arises. By knowing where you traded or sold a book, you may perhaps be able to recover it should it become of interest to you again. By keeping a record of the cost of the book, you can determine a fair sale or trade value.

The *Soldat* Collector's and Collector's Events Agenda

Setting a goal for your collecting saves time and money. Setting overall collecting objectives and then breaking these objectives into a workable timetable allows for a focused and planned approach to collecting.

The agendas provide work sheets for your objectives. The area headings are self-explanatory. The agendas can help you remain on target towards your collecting objectives even when you are engaged in the "close combat" of a trading event.

Summary

I encourage you to make photocopies of *The Soldat Combat Uniform Collector's Planner*. I am providing them for you use as a buyer of *Soldat*. As you grow with your hobby, you will find that this log will grow with you. As time passes, the value of these records will appreciate.

By photocopying these pages, you can make your *Soldat Planner* fit your needs. The arrangement of the pages if up to you. If you have a sizable collection and have no records, I encourage you to begin recording your items to the best of your ability and to continue record-keeping in this format.

I wish you all good collecting!

Cyrus A. Lee

Soldat Collection Information Log

Item:____

Presently in my Collection: ___Yes ___No

Value of this Item: $________

This item was ___ purchased or ___traded from ________________
_________________ on ____/____/____ at ___________________
for a value of $________ (if foreign currency was used for the
purchase note the type and rate of exchange against the U.S.
dollar here: _______ at _______ to the U.S. dollar). If traded, note item
given: ____
This item was ___ purchased from or ___ was a gift from a veteran. The
former owner is/was   ___________________________________
who held the rank of _________________ in the _____________
during the years from _______ to _______. This item was ___ issued to
or ____ taken at ___________________ in _______.

Identifying Description, or Characteristics of this Item

Marking Code/Numbers: ____________________________________
Condition: ____

Modifications, Changes or Damage Unique to this Item: _________

____
____
____
____
____
____
____
____
____

Historical Information: ____________________________________

____
____
____

This Item was ___ sold to ___ traded to _____________________

____

Amount Received:____

Name: _______________________________________

Collecting Interest(s): _______________________________________

____

Address: _______________________________________

____

____

____

Telephone: _______ - _______ - _______ - _______

Notes: _______________________________________

____

____

____

____

____

____

____

Name of Firm or Person: _______________________________

Type of Business: _______________________________

Address: _______________________________

____

____

Business
Card
Here

Telephone: _______ - _______ - _______ - _______

Notes: _______________________________

____

____

____

____

____

Soldat Veteran's Roster

Name: ____

Former Rank: _______________________________________

Address: ____

____

____

Telephone: _____ - _____ - _____ - _______________

Date of Birth: _____ / _____ / _____

Units Served With:

1. _______________________ Dates: ___/___ To ___/___

2. _______________________ Dates: ___/___ To ___/___

3. _______________________ Dates: ___/___ To ___/___

Major Campaigns and Actions:

1. _______________________ Dates: ___/___ To ___/___

2. _______________________ Dates: ___/___ To ___/___

3. _______________________ Dates: ___/___ To ___/___

Awards and Decorations:

1. __________ 2. __________ 3. __________

4. __________ 5. __________ 6. __________

Items Still in Veteran's Possession:

1. __________________ Condition: __________ Value:$ ______

2. __________________ Condition: __________ Value:$ ______

3. __________________ Condition: __________ Value:$ ______

4. __________________ Condition: __________ Value:$ ______

5. __________________ Condition: __________ Value:$ ______

Veteran's Historical Background on Items:

1. ____

____

____

____

____

____

____

____

2. ____

____

____

____

____

____

____

____

3. ____

____

____

____

____

____

____

____

4. ____

____

____

____

____

____

____

____

____

Is the Veteran willing to Sell, Trade or give the Items as Gifts?____
If the Veteran will Sell or Trade, what is the Price or Item needed
to complete the transaction:_______________________________________
If the Veteran is not willing to part with the Items, will he or she
allow photographs? _____Yes _____No
The **Initial Date of Contact** with the Veteran was ____/____/____
Dates for Follow-up Contact:
1.___/___/___**Notes:**_______________________________________
2.___/___/___**Notes:**_______________________________________
3.___/___/___**Notes:**_______________________________________
4.___/___/___**Notes:**_______________________________________
5.___/___/___**Notes:**_______________________________________

Gift/Correspondence Costs:
1.Item:_____________________________**Cost:**___________
2.Item:_____________________________**Cost:**___________
3.Item:_____________________________**Cost:**___________
4.Item:_____________________________**Cost:**___________

Soldat Collector's Bibliography Log

Reference Source For: ___________________________________

Title: ___________________________________

Author: ___________________________________

Publisher: ___________________________________

of ___________________________________

Purchased or Traded from: ___________________________________

on ____/____/____ for the value of $______________ (if traded,
note item given______________).

Notes: ___________________________________

____

____

____

Traded or Sold to:______________________________on___/___/___
for a value of $________________ (if traded, note item received

______________________________________).

My Overall Collecting Objective(s):

A.____
B.____
C.____
D.____
E.____
F.____

The Overall Collecting Objective(s) for 19___:

A.____
B.____
C.____
D.____
E.____

Major Collecting Events to Attend in 19___:

1.______________________________________ Date:___/___/___
2.______________________________________ Date:___/___/___
3.______________________________________ Date:___/___/___
4.______________________________________ Date:___/___/___
5.______________________________________ Date:___/___/___
6.______________________________________ Date:___/___/___
7.______________________________________ Date:___/___/___
8.______________________________________ Date:___/___/___
9.______________________________________ Date:___/___/___
10.______________________________________ Date:___/___/___
11.______________________________________ Date:___/___/___
12.______________________________________ Date:___/___/___
13.______________________________________ Date:___/___/___
14.______________________________________ Date:___/___/___
15.______________________________________ Date:___/___/___

Soldat Collector's Event Agenda

Event:____

Date:___/___/___ Point of Contact:_____________________

Address:____

____

____

Overall Collecting Objectives for this Event:

A.____

B.____

C.____

Specific Collecting Objectives for this Event:

A.____

B.____

C.____

Primary Collection Items to Buy or Trade:

A._______________________________Target Price:$__________

B._______________________________Target Price:$__________

C._______________________________Target Price:$__________

Items to Sell or Trade:

1._______________________________Value $_______________

2._______________________________Value $_______________

3._______________________________Value $_______________

Secondary Collection Items to Buy or Trade:

1._______________________________Target Price:$__________

2._______________________________Target Price:$__________

3._______________________________Target Price:$__________

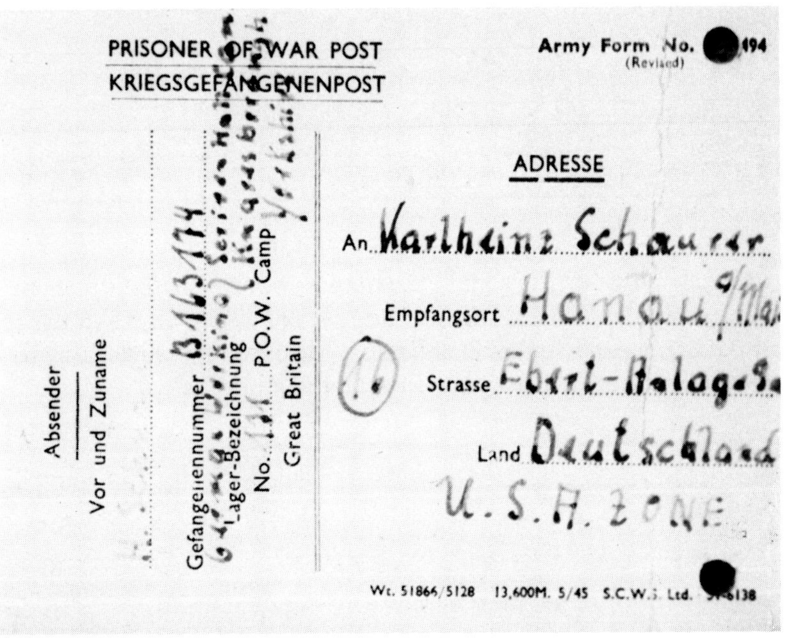

The last field post home. This P.O.W. postcard was mailed at the expense of the victors. For the soldier and family who survived the war, a very emotional piece of mail.

I continue to collect and study the uniforms, equipment, weapons and artifacts of the German soldier of the Second World War. As my research continues, my collection and interests are focusing on the soldiers of the Panzerkorps Grossdeutschland, their individual stories, uniforms, equipment, weapons, and memorabilia. This focus will culminate in *Soldat*: Volume V: Equipping the Soldiers of Panzerkorps Grossdeutschland 1939-1945.

While working as a teacher in Germany, I am able to learn more about the German soldier and his homeland. This location allows time to be spent visiting and researching European battlefields, meeting with veterans and searching out collectible items for inclusion in future volumes of *Soldat*.

Aside from writing and researching, I have begun to speak publicly about writing and researching books on the German Army soldier of World War II. I hope that I will be able to impart some of my experiences in collecting, researching and writing to fellow collectors, historians, writers and students.

Cyrus and his colleague Kaiser Friedrich Barbarrossa work on Vol. V of *Soldat*.